The Cat Who Read the Mail

*sixteen amazing stories
about our mysterious
bond with animals*

The Cat
Who Read
the Mail

*sixteen amazing stories
about our mysterious
bond with animals*

Elinor Donahue

Copyright © 2005 by Elinor Donahue.

ISBN: Softcover 1-59926-414-5

All rights reserved. No part of this book may be reproduced or transmitted in any form or by any means, electronic or mechanical, including photocopying, recording, or by any information storage and retrieval system, without permission in writing from the copyright owner.

This book was printed in the United States of America.

Cover design by David Linton

To order additional copies of this book, contact:
Xlibris Corporation
1-888-795-4274
www.Xlibris.com
Orders@Xlibris.com

30176

Contents

Introduction 9

The Cat Who Read the Mail 13

Bob: The Recycling Cat 17

Oliver Augustus 21

Call Me Rexy 24

Skunk: The Easy Rider 29

The Dog Who Mourned at Ground Zero 33

The Soft Underbelly of Roo 38

A Prince, a Horse and Maslow Too 42

A Cry in the Night—and That's Not All 50

Is That You, Malibu? 55

Glimpse of a Ghost 59

Being Scruffy 62

How to Fetch a Human 67

What a Difference a Name Makes 71

Rafting on the River Styx 75

The Dog in the Window 80

**With deep gratitude for Cherie
and with love for my companions on this journey**

Introduction

Something Extraordinary

These stories are about animals and their part in something extraordinary, something unexpected. Each presents us with an *aha!* moment—if not of crystal clarity, then surely of wonder.

At the core of each story is an experience, an event, which is out of the range of what we take to be possible. All accounts are factual, from real life. Some are simply not explainable by ordinary rational processes. In that sense they are stories that amaze us.

But these are not the familiar "amazing animal" stories.

We know that animals do heroic things. A mother cat will run into a burning building to save her kittens, for instance. And the participation of animals in the work and play of human life is a given. Dogs herd, guard, assist the disabled, rescue disaster victims and sniff land mines and illegal trade. Horses have long been our dependable servants, plowing fields, transporting people and cargo and charging into human battles.

These stories, however, are about a different kind of extraordinary animal behavior. You are invited to come with eyes wide open—and allow a new focus to emerge. Much as when the eye becomes accustomed to a dark room, stay long enough and a shape begins to form.

One of these happenings came upon my friend, Robyn, and that is what started this book. When her dog, Malibu, died, she called to tell me about it—and added that something bizarre was now happening with her cat. The laid-back Whip had taken on the habits of the departed Malibu. When Robyn came into the kitchen early one morning a few days after the dog died, for instance, she found the floor cabinets had all been opened—just as Malibu had done nightly, foraging for treats. The story, which she initially described as "too weird," was out of her realm—out of the daily world we wake up in, go to work in, feed our families in.

Looking for others who might have had similar experiences, Robyn asked around. So did I. There was story upon story. Collected here, they emerge as part *Dr. Doolittle*, part *Twilight Zone* and part Ripley's *Believe It or Not*. But they are all real life experiences.

To get into them, what I invite here is a mind that says *maybe* or *yes*. Either view will take you to the place where these stories come from. The fact is we can't comprehend these events with a skeptical distance or our usual intellectual processes. And I attempt no explanations.

But animals doing the extraordinary—those stories can penetrate us. They fascinate, comfort, agitate, and settle. They make their way into the crevices of our thinking and our capacity for wonder.

We're looking here at animals and the fabulous. We're talking about elevated events that occurred in the very much grounded lives of human beings. As such, they make us realize that our sense of what is real and possible and happening everywhere, every day, may be far too limited.

Fabulous stories, yes. But more fable than fact? I don't believe so. The individuals who report these events were asked for their stories. They did not proffer or push them. Where they prefer privacy, I have changed their names. I view each of these people as thoroughly credible. No la-la land dwellers here. All are people with jobs to do, families to care for, households to run, lives that are full. They are in no need of acclaim or attention.

When possible, I've checked the stories with anyone else who was present. When no one else was there, I've relied on my assessment of the demeanor, sensibility and intention of the person.

While animals do not speak our language, they speak unequivocally through action. Through movement. Alfred Adler, the Austrian psychiatrist, said, "Trust only movement. Life happens at the level of events not of words." So do not trust my words but see the events. Consider what is unspoken but directly communicated.

This is not a book of answers. Or perhaps the questions are the answer. The poet Rainer Maria Rilke said in his *Letters to a Young Poet*, "Learn to love the questions." One question that comes up is what precipitates such events. These are often stories of companion animals and many of them seem to emanate from the bond of that relationship. The bond of a beloved person and a beloved pet. Like the cat that patrols the neighborhood for rubbish—make that recyclable goods—and brings home to the family something just right for the moment. But that is not always the case. Certainly Rexy, the dog rescued by Paul, can't be accounted for that way. Paul and Rexy had never met before.

Some of these stories are about what happens after an animal is departed. It's the memory of Skunk whose owner, on horseback, was abruptly stopped at a bush where newly hatched butterflies appeared, just as forecast. It's the mourned Oliver Augustus, who just maybe used a mourning dove to tell his grieving humans, "Hey, it's all right where I am."

This, then, is a book about wonder. The moment of the inswept breath—the *aha!* that catches us unaware. In all of these stories we are invited to leap the boundaries of what we define as believable and stretch our narrow shafts of knowing. And we are asked to recognize the intelligence and the cognizance of animals and their participation with us in something larger.

Yet these moments can look perfectly ordinary. As they do in the work of Liz Teal, animal-assisted therapy worker who with her dog, Annie, walked Ground Zero's neighborhood after September 11.

What gives power to these stories is that they are for the good. Numinous with something positive. They invite us to know the enduring power of attending, listening, loving and allowing for the ineffable.

We may believe, or we may not. But again and again, the unexplainable finds its way in. Into lives like yours and mine, Robyn's, Joel's, Dawn's. Suffused through it all is the embedded mystery in the joy and suffering of life and death. And the clear unhesitating part that animals take in that flow—willing to show us that more is afoot than we can see or know. When that happens, animals take us beyond our expectations, allowing us to catch a glimpse of where we might be.

The Cat Who Read the Mail

Everything started at the kitchen door. For all the family comings and goings at the Willis house in rural Pennsylvania, this was the main entrance. Routinely, Jean would be the first one home after work. She and her husband, Bill, both police officers, were on different shifts. Jean would grab the mail from the outside box, giving it a quick glance. Junk flyers, bills, sometimes a card for her daughter, mail for Bill. The usual. It could wait. She'd toss the stack on the kitchen table.

Then one day something changed. When Jean came home, there on the rug by the kitchen door lay a piece of mail shredded and chewed into bite-size pieces. A professional-grade cat hit. Okay, Jean thought. One of them—there were five cats in the household—has a new game afoot.

What the cat had chosen to attack, kill and deposit at the door for front-and-center attention was an insurance check. Addressed to Bill.

A few days later, Jean came in the kitchen door as usual to find another mutilated letter on the rug. This time a paycheck. Bill's paycheck. Now the pace picked up. The next quarry dropped at the door: a receipt Bill needed for reimbursement at work. Ripped to shreds.

Who Is the Mail Mauler?

Now on a regular basis, selectively extracted from the mail stack on the table, ripped to bits and deposited by the door was Bill's mail. And only Bill's mail.

"At first I thought it was just random," Jean says. "But then I saw it wasn't just the colorful mail the cat targeted. It wasn't the junk mail—the credit card applications or the supermarket flyers. The cat never touched those or my mail or my daughter's." The cat only went after mail that counted with Bill. "It seemed the more value it had, the more intent the cat was on shredding it," Jean noticed.

Okay, she thought, the cat is sorting out Bill's mail. "Don't ask me how," she says. "It wasn't like Bill would come home, pick it up and lay his mail aside. No. I got home first and Bill hadn't touched this mail. But the cat would pick

13

out one of his letters and shred it on the kitchen rug where I'd be sure to see it as soon as I came in."

Question was, which of the five cats was doing this?

After a couple of weeks of ravaged mail, Bill started taking his mail upstairs to his room and placing it on his dresser, protecting it from cat attack. "He was starting to get annoyed. But I wasn't sure what was happening," Jean recalls.

Samson Uncovered

Then, sitting in the living room one night, Jean out of the corner of her eye saw their gray tiger-striped cat, Samson, running downstairs with a piece of paper in his mouth. Into the kitchen he went with his prey. He dropped the letter by the door, positioned the piece between his paws to cock it up slightly—then dug his teeth into it, ripped away and spat it out on the rug. Bill's mail.

No stealthy deed was this. No surreptitious stashing of the evidence behind the sofa. No. This was in-your-face. "Oh," Jean thought. "Samson is mad at you, Bill, isn't he."

"Samson is a lovable cat," Jean says with matter-of-fact detachment. A barn cat taken in to be a mouser for the house (this is the country), Samson eventually moved indoors as did every other cat the Willises had. "He goes out occasionally, but is content to be inside most of the time. He'd never done anything like this. And it wasn't like I thought of Samson as 'my' cat. He loved me up, but he loved Bill up too. Bill was never abusive to him, even after the cat started shredding his mail."

Deciding she needed to see the cat's whole sequence of action, Jean started to watch Samson's modus operandi closely. Bill had by now taken to closing his bedroom door since the cat might lay waste to his mail no matter where it was. So Jean set up an opportunity for Samson.

She opened Bill's bedroom door one evening. Then watching from across the hall, Jean saw Samson creep into Bill's room. He sniffed around, pawed at the rug where Bill had tossed his clothes, sniffed the bed, hopped up on the dresser, grabbed a piece mail with his teeth, jumped off, ran downstairs to the kitchen door—and sat there shredding his prey.

Something Is Different

Jean took the cat to the vet. "Obviously the cat's upset about something," the vet offered. "I thought, well, yeah, Bill has changed his schedule. He's working nights and extra shifts. Makes sense that the cat is unhappy because Bill isn't home as much as he used to be."

"Try some vitamin B," the vet suggested. Jean did. Nothing changed.

It was getting freaky—and not cute anymore. "Bill was quite angry that he had to call the insurance company and ask them to reissue that check."

Enter Anita.

Anita Curtis, an animal communicator, happened to be enrolled in the art class Jean was taking. In casual conversation over the course of weeks, Jean began to get the drift of what Anita did. "I really didn't know what animal communication was all about, but on the off chance that Anita really could talk to animals, I said to her, 'Anita, maybe you can help me figure out why the cat is doing this.'"

Jean handed Anita a picture of Samson—with his white face and black-rimmed eyes. Anita closed her eyes and was silent a minute. Then she said: "Well, the cat says things are really different in the house. He's upset. Bill is not coming home when Samson thinks he should."

"That's right," Jean thought. "Bill is working extra shifts, two jobs really. The change doesn't sit right with the cat." Anita went on. "Well, it's not only that."

Jean smiles about it today: "Anita was very tactful." Anita continued: "Bill smells different," she said. "He has a smell to him that isn't the same. Maybe he's been around somebody who smokes."

Finally Anita added the piercing insight. "The cat tells me it smells perfume and it isn't yours because you don't wear perfume. In cat parlance, he thinks Bill is catting around."

The Chuckle Runs Dry

"You know what," Jean recalls, "even that didn't strike a chord with me. It never crossed my mind. I thought—right. A lady looks at a picture of my cat—a cat that's nowhere around—and talks to it. And the cat talks back. I'm getting a chuckle out of all this."

"I went home that night after talking to Anita. Bill happened to call from work. I said jokingly, 'Hey, guess what the cat said today! Well, there's this woman in art class who says she talks to animals—and Samson says you've been out fooling around.'"

Bill's reaction? "He went ballistic," as Jean describes it. "Off the deep end. Now *that* perked up my senses. I thought, wait a minute. I wasn't being ugly. Or yelling. I was laughing about it."

"That's when I called in my friend Rosemary. I said, 'You've got to watch this with me and see what's happening here.'" Together they replicated the sleuthing Jean had set up for Samson before. "We opened the door to Bill's bedroom, spied from across the hall—and saw Samson go in. He repeated the ritual. Pawed the floor, sniffed the bed, jumped up on the dresser, grabbed a piece of paper in his mouth and ran downstairs to the kitchen. We followed him. He chewed it up and spat it out on the rug by the door."

That's also when Jean started a little investigation of her own. And found? "The cat was right. Bill was seeing somebody else. The cat had picked it up right from the start, began selecting Bill's mail from the stack on the kitchen table and shredding it on the kitchen floor so I'd be sure to see it as soon as I came in."

"I never thought of Samson as 'my cat' but apparently he felt protective of me," Jean says.

It Started with the Cat

Today if someone asks Jean how her marriage broke up, she says, "Well, it started with the cat."

After Bill departed, Samson quickly returned to his normal behavior. "He hasn't chewed a piece of paper in the two years since Bill has been gone," Jean says. "Samson is lying here on the bed, the most lovable cat in the world. He now finds better things to use his kitty time for than feline detective work. Like chasing mice and watching birds."

And with a new man in Jean's life now, Samson isn't bothered a bit. But the running joke in the house is, "If Samson ever starts chewing your mail . . ."

Bob: The Recycling Cat

Not Just Any Rubbish

You could tell what was happening in the Campbells' life by the kind of trash the cat dragged in.

At first it was fairly standard feline scavenging. Not that the garbage ever lacked a certain *idiosyncratic* quality. No, right from the start, Bob showed a definite bias for *recyclables*—a not-so-fast-here reconsideration of the discarded. Bob prowling the neighborhood was a cat on a mission. And if it took some deft heisting from the trash to carry out that mission, well, you do what you have to do.

Holly and Jake had just moved from Seattle to Oregon and found the perfect setting for their lifestyle. Their new hometown offered all the outdoor enticements of the Northwest—and the bonus of sunny weather. The neighborhood drew them, too, with houses built in the Craftsman style—complete with front porches and an old-timey feel.

Starting Over

It was a new state, a new start. Holly became pregnant—to their special delight after fertility struggles. Time for a kitty now, said the couple. And since the pregnancy might be twins, how about *two* cats. The Animal Rescue League had plenty, but two barn cats, black with white paws and white chests, about seven months old, had just been dropped off by a pickup truck. Docile and friendly, they won their way home with the Campbells. One cat was named Billy, the other, Bob.

Look alike though they might, Billy and Bob showed completely different personalities. "If he were a human, Billy would be sitting on the fence chewing a piece of straw contemplating the world," says Holly. "Bob, on the other hand, would be thinking about what little industrious thing he's going to do."

17

Industrious indeed. Holly soon saw Bob running across the yard with his prey gripped between his teeth. It was a blue bottle cap. Bob's travel path was through two cat doors. The first door led through the garage into the back yard; the next, from the yard into the house. Bob would deposit the collectible on the kitchen floor if Holly was there. And if she wasn't, he'd tote it up to the bedroom.

Soon Bob moved up to bigger quarry. A soda cup. A plastic water bottle. Next Holly heard a "crumple, crumple, crumple" sound. It was Bob dragging in a whole section of newspaper. Or as much of it as he could pull through the cat doors.

Really Prime Garbage

With the knack of the kill now mastered, Bob scouted the neighborhood for really prime garbage. Never animal prey, only trash. A neighborhood still under construction was oh-so-ripe with potential for a crafty hunter like Bob. In came a bag of bolts. Then bagged lunches from a workmen's site. Drop it in front of Holly if she's right there in the kitchen, of course. If not, drag it up to the bedroom where she and Jake won't miss this prize.

Being a sensitive cat, Bob saw he could be even more useful to Holly and Jake now that they were expecting a child. He started dragging in toys. A little girl's hairband. A child's mitten.

When Holly lost the pregnancy, it weighed heavily on the couple. "We'd been in a painful place for so long," Holly says of their long hopes and years in fertility clinics.

With family feeling and a hunter's prowess, Bob made an offering. The poem.

"He dropped it on the bedroom floor," says Holly. "It was a single sheet, like the card stock you find in magazines for subscription renewals." On it was a poem called, "To Thine Own Self" by James Dillet Freeman. "The poem was about longing—longing for something other than what you have," as Holly sees it. "It was about a mountain by a lake. The mountain always wanted to be as placid and serene as the lake and the lake longed to be as tall and majestic as the mountain. Yet each as it was came together to form a unity."

The point Holly took was, "What you have is beautiful. I think we were losing sight of that in our lives, and it was appropriate for this time in my life to get that perspective," she says.

A Little Something for the Baby

Holly and Jake decided to pursue adoption. "We started the process and all the home study interviews had been completed. We were just waiting to hear if we had a child," Holly says.

That was when Bob clicked right in and started bringing home a child's things again. "It was stuffed animals—a little dinosaur, a stuffed duck. Then a child's homework. Maybe a first grader's. Then in the bedroom one night we heard Bob trot in with the 'Eeehhhh, Ehhhh, Ehhhh' cry that means, 'I've got something.' It was a hand puppet. A little green worm with bulging eyes and a pink mouth."

The call came unexpectedly. A baby had been born in the hospital and did the Campbells want him? Yes, indeed they did. Jason arrived at the house in June. It was spring and life was opening anew. The season of birth and renewal and expansion in the Campbell family had begun.

Wouldn't some gardening equipment be appropriate, Bob seemed to think. Off he went into the neighborhood to hunt for tools to support the nesting that was underway. Back he came with gardening gloves. A pack of seeds. A roll of green gardening jute for tying up drooping plants. Plastic markers for plants. And a recipe for gingerbread on an envelope.

While he takes care of family first, Bob doesn't lose sight of larger community issues. Jake, in fact, is in the recycling business, just as Bob is. When Jake was getting his business started, Bob endorsed it by dragging home several recycling leaflets and a flyer that said, "Recycle your phone books." Regularly he pulled plenty of crumpled newspaper and paper bags through the cat doors.

But Bob doesn't push his agenda. "He drops it on the floor and that's it," says Holly. "He'll flop down next to it if I'm there," she says, "and I'll go over and pet him to thank him for keeping the neighborhood tidy."

So diligent is he at the task—and so famous for it in the neighborhood—that a local TV station came by to broadcast his story. Bob instantly became something of a recycling celebrity. When Jake posted Bob's picture at a home show where he was advertising his recycling business, he promised a tee shirt to anyone who recognized this certain black-and-white cat. Soon Jake racked up a tee shirt bill. Lots of people recognized him. "Oh, that's Bob, the Recycling Cat!"

At times the retrieval expeditions are outright theft. Like the pepper plant that Holly found by the cat door. A foot tall in a plastic container, it just didn't fit through the hole. Holly returned it to its owner next door, who put it out of cat reach, she thought. But no match was this for Bob's scavenging skills. Next day the plant appeared again at the cat door.

At times Bob can be entirely practical. Consider the phone bill he dropped off in the bedroom just when it was due.

Holly has started listening with new respect for what the cat knows. When she is going to fly, which she does frequently in her job as a corporate consultant, she pays attention to Bob's behavior. "If he's clingy or nervous, I take that into consideration. I think he's sort of plugged in."

Oliver Augustus

The Cat and the Dove

It was a warm autumn day and Dawn Hayman left the back door open as she swept the kitchen floor. Putting the broom down, she stepped into the living room for maybe 45 seconds, then came back to the kitchen.

There it was.

A mourning dove. Calmly standing in front of the refrigerator—and staring directly at Dawn. Planted exactly where Oliver Augustus the cat used to sit and bask in the warm air that blew from under the fridge.

"I froze in my tracks," Dawn recalls. "First I thought, 'Oh boy, I've got to get this bird out of here before it flies and hits a window and breaks its neck.'"

But the bird was in no such panic. "As soon as it saw me, it just stared at me. Then it slowly turned around and very casually walked some 30 feet across the kitchen to the back door and went out." Dawn followed the bird out the door.

"When that dove looked me straight in the eye, I immediately thought of Oliver Augustus," Dawn says.

Once outside, the bird ambled over to the large flat stone that marked Oliver's grave and sat there. Sat on exactly the spot where two days before Dawn and Bonnie Reynolds, co-founders of Spring Farm CARES, a haven for horses in Clinton, New York, had buried the house cat, Oliver Augustus. They had deliberately chosen this precise location under the bird feeder, and marked the grave with a flat rock until they could put up a suitable memorial.

As the mourning dove serenely parked itself on Oliver Augustus' grave, Dawn ran to get Bonnie to show her the bird. "When we came back, it was gone."

Dawn remembers saying out loud, "Thank you."

The Perfect Perch

"What made me think instantly of the cat when I saw the bird in front of the refrigerator was the way Oliver used to chase those mourning doves all the time. He had this absolute fixation on mourning doves."

Oliver had a sentry's perfect perch for the game. Crouched in the sink in front of the kitchen window, he could eyeball the bird feeder that hung just seven or eight feet away. "He'd hunker down in the sink where the birds couldn't see him. Then as soon as the mourning doves gathered to peck at the seeds scattered from the feeder—after they'd all landed—he'd spring up and pounce at the glass and scare them away."

"It was his favorite thing," Dawn recalls. "He didn't bother with the rest of the birds, but those mourning doves he loved to get going. I think he just loved the fluttery sound they made when they took off."

The Call of the Wild

Oliver Augustus had departed from the planet unexpectedly. Five years old, luxuriantly longhaired in black and white fur, his eyes circled in black markings that dripped mascara-like down his cheeks, Oliver was content with the indoor life. A splash in the toilet, a daredevil walk on a narrow ledge, a nose-to-nose endearment with Dawn or Bonnie followed by a cocky turn of his head—"to make you laugh," these were adventures enough, the makings of a good day.

But occasionally the wild would call. A quick bolt out the door for a romp in the leaves? Irresistible! Oliver seized the chance when he could. As he did that autumn morning when the leaves swirled and beckoned.

"But he wouldn't go very far, and usually we could scoop him up quickly. He'd never go off and disappear," says Dawn.

"We saw him zipping around but he wouldn't let us catch him that day. He took off chasing leaves under some bushes and we couldn't get him out. We said, 'Oh, he'll come right back.' But he didn't. Then we had to go out to pick up a horse in our horse trailer and bring it here to Spring Farm—and we couldn't find Oliver when we were ready to go. We were gone several hours. On the way back we were talking about how when we got home we were sure he'd be sitting there at the door waiting for us."

"As soon as we came up the road we saw a cat lying by the side of the road. It was just getting dark and the headlights caught the sight of a white belly—just like Oliver Augustus'. We knew instantly," says Dawn.

If Only . . .

"We were beside ourselves with grief. We thought if only we had searched for him more, or tried to catch him a little harder, maybe he wouldn't have been out." Unresolved and remorseful, Dawn and Bonnie buried Oliver Augustus under the feeder he had enjoyed stalking so mischievously from the kitchen window.

Not that they were waiting for a consoling signal, but Dawn and Bonnie had come to know that reminders from departed pets occur frequently. "Often after an animal dies at Spring Farm, some kind of message will come to let us know the animal is okay. It can be just some reassuring thing or something that makes us suddenly think of the animal and laugh. We see it again and again at Spring Farm. With all the animals we've had over the years, we watch for it when we lose an animal."

"Still, when I see it, it hits me with a wow, even if I'm expecting it," Dawn says.

How does Dawn know that the mourning dove was about Oliver Augustus? "When the bird stared at me from in front of the refrigerator, it instantly brought tears to my eyes and I felt Oliver Augustus emotionally. It was just a knowing. I knew Oliver Augustus was okay."

"It was a symbol that got our attention. I mean it's pretty rare to have a bird just walk in your house, look you in the eye, and calmly saunter out to sit on your cat's grave." She muses in retrospect, "It so fit him."

Call Me Rexy

"Everyone I tell this story to thinks I'm making it up."

Paul Tharp is the manager of Horse Haven at Best Friends Animal Society in Kanab, Utah—and *not* the kind of a guy who makes things up. In cowboy hat and faded jeans, he looks like a western wrangler—which is what he is at Best Friends, the nation's largest sanctuary for abused and abandoned animals. His day there is filled with tending some 25 horses, "fixing things for their care." This is a man who knows horses instinctively, as you can see when he nuzzles one to his face.

Paul, along with his staff, has turned the horse department at Best Friends into a peak-operating haven for horses that need either a way station or a permanent place to live. The daily routine is mucking stalls, cleaning water troughs, giving medication, fixing fence, and bringing in hay. Making sure everything is, in Paul's words, "up to speed" for the horses.

At the same time the horse department is always looking for the right adoptive homes for the animals in their care. Emphasis is on the word *right*. "That is our commitment to the horses," Paul says. "No matter what, they're going to have a good home. Whether it's here or someplace else."

Before coming to Best Friends, Paul had just retired from a career in the Air Force. But his work at Best Friends "matches my personality better," he says. After all, he'd been around horses all his life—ever since he was a boy helping on his grandfather's farm.

The Best Friends connection started a few years back when Paul, his wife and their son took a vacation visit to the sanctuary. Here, deep in the red-rock country of Angel Canyon, circled by Grand Canyon, Zion National Park and Bryce Canyon, they knew they'd found where they wanted to be.

When they went home, Paul put in an application to Best Friends. Six months later a job opened up: manager of the horse department. "We're going!" Paul's wife said, though they had planned to wait until their son graduated from high school before moving to Kanab. "This is where her heart was," says Paul. And Paul's heart? "I wouldn't want to be anywhere else but here in the canyon.

I have a hard time *not* being here," he says, so natural to him are the animals, the land, the "real peaceful feeling."

But none of that prepared him for the ride with Rexy.

Picking up a Passenger

"We—myself and two others—were away at a hoof-care clinic," Paul begins the story. "It's specialty training on certain shoes to put on the horses to prevent disease and help with conditions like lameness."

While at the clinic, they arranged to bring back to Best Friends a dog that had been used in anesthesia research. The dog was a stray before that, ending up in a shelter and then finally a research lab.

Hoof-care clinic over, the Best Friends caravan started back to the sanctuary. Paul and the dog shared a compact white Toyota, with the dog in the back seat. The others followed in a truck and trailer, hauling the horses they'd brought to the clinic and a pig they'd picked up for a new life at Best Friends.

"When we first got in the car, oh man, he was one timid dog," Paul remembers. With flat, white fur, a square pit-bull-like head, a pink nose and pink-rimmed eyes, he was a 60-pound mixed breed, maybe four to five years old.

"He would sit in the back and look at me with a blank stare. He was frozen still, not knowing what was happening," Paul surmises. "Just consider everything that had happened in his life before."

"I had some snacks with me and when we took off I gave him a few. But he wasn't sure what to do with them. He kind of sniffed them and lay there next to them. I said, 'Go ahead and eat them'—and I ate some, so finally he knew he could eat them."

But this was one intent dog, watching every move Paul made. "If I just reached over and did something, like take a drink of coffee, his head and eyes would follow me."

Along the way, the caravan stopped to get some lunch. The others went into the restaurant, but Paul stayed outside with the dog. "I thought, 'Well, he probably needs to get out and go to the bathroom.' But the dog was so afraid I had to pick him up and carry him over to the grass. He just lay there and shook." Paul stops reflectively. "So I got him to get up and take a couple of steps—then he just lay down and shook. It was like he'd never been out on grass before. He never did go to the bathroom. He wouldn't bark, wouldn't wag his tail."

The Passenger Has a Name

"We spent the whole hour out there sittin' in the grass, talking. I was just telling him, 'Hey, you know, it's okay. It's a nice day. Grass isn't going to hurt you. Cars going by aren't going to hurt you. I'm not going to hurt you or anything.' And I'd pet him and just kind of small talk to him."

"All this time I'd been calling him different names, trying to figure out what would be a good one. I think I called him Sam or Fred a few times. Names of dogs I'd had and just names for dogs. But he never responded to any of them." In the research lab, the dog had only a number.

"So after lunch we got back in the car and were going down the road. He was just there in the back seat, sometimes sniffing my ear. I was just driving along and I said, 'Well, you know, we've been together all this trip and I still don't know what to call you. I'm thinking of all these names, but what do *you* want to be called?' You know how you do when you're just talking."

"So I'm driving along and about ten minutes later I turned around to see what he was up to."

When Paul looked at the back seat, his eyes were drawn to the rear passenger side window. On it was written the name REXY.

"He was sittin' by the window, looking at me, panting like dogs do and bobbing his head."

"You know how dogs get a wet nose and leave nose prints on your window. It was like he used his nose and wrote his name."

What kind of lettering? "Actually for a dog it was very good," Paul laughs. "It was all capital letters. About three to four inches high, covering probably an eight-inch span. All individually made letters. All solid lines. The only dotted line was where you'd put the leg down for the R. There was a little space between the leg and the circle for the P. The E was like a big curved C with a line in the middle for an E. And the X was really good. The Y was a little shaky on the tail of the Y."

"I had to keep looking a long time. I couldn't believe it was on there. I was trying to drive and at the same time look back at the window."

And the dog? How did he behave after Paul looked around and saw the name REXY on the window? "He was a little more relaxed after. He had a softer look on his face. He was sitting upright over by the window and just kind of looking at me like, 'This is what I want to be called. Aren't I a good boy?' And he had that soft look in his eye."

"It seemed like he was saying, 'This is what I'm trying to tell you.'"

Did Paul hear any unusual movement in the back seat when this was going on? "Nothing. He was just sitting there like he'd been the whole trip. And in ten minutes, maybe 15 at the most, he did this. I wish I could have seen that—but I guess that's something I wasn't supposed to see."

"I tell you when I did see it, I sure did get goose bumps. It was like, man, this is just too strange."

Pretty soon Rexy lay down and went to sleep. But instead of being curled up in a tight ball in the corner as before, now he stretched out and took up the whole back seat.

How the Car Felt

The atmosphere in the car changed after that.

"It's really hard to describe. It was kind of scary, a kind of excited, mystical feeling, I guess." Paul is silent a moment, recalling it. "Unbelievable. It's like I can't believe he did that. It was like, that's really cool, but how did you do that?" Paul shakes his head. "Is something going on back there I don't know about? It must have been, because it happened."

"It just felt really strange in the car. I had goose bumps. But it was kind of a happy thing going on there too. Have you ever been on a roller coaster and you take one of those big dips—and it feels like your stomach goes up? It was like that. It's fear but it's excitement too. It's just hard to explain."

Did Paul ever think he was seeing things? "Nope, never did. I just thought, this has to be what he wants to be called."

"There's something that made this happen and I'm not sure what it was, but it felt like something really important happened there."

"We had another three to four hours to go after that. Rexy would get up and look and he'd sniff my ear. I'd feed him a few potato chips and he'd eat them. He just seemed kind of more relaxed."

When they rolled into Best Friends, Paul immediately called in a second opinion. Just to get a reality check. Pulling into the horse department, he said to one of the women on the staff, "I want you to come look at the car and tell me what you think this window says." She did. "Looks like Rexy," she responded. "I said, 'That's what I thought too. You know that dog wrote that on there?' She said, 'You're full of it. You wrote that on there.' I said, 'I swear I didn't.' She thought I must have written it on there before I came down."

"I just said, believe it or not, it's true. That happened."

Room in the Mind

Though Paul doesn't attempt to explain how it could happen, he does credit life in Angel Canyon in Utah and his work with the animals at Best Friends with creating a mindset that allows him to see more of what is happening around him.

"There's something about this canyon that has changed me," he acknowledges. "Changed the way I think about things, even relationships with people. It's given me more of a peaceful feeling. I think if I hadn't been here doing this that this would never have happened with Rexy. And what happened with Rexy has helped me relate better to the other animals. Because I know if I pay attention, I'm gonna see something. I may not see it for a week or a month, but I know I'm gonna see something if I just pay attention."

"I think many times we try to guess what the animal is thinking. We have in our heads, 'I bet he wants to go here or there.' And you're not listening. But if you just kind of make your mind real blank, then it will happen."

"So I think when I said, 'What do *you* want to be called?' I just kind of let everything go out of *my* head waiting to see what his answer was going to be. Instead of me trying to think of a name for him."

"Rexy is not even a name I'd think of. He definitely had his own name picked out."

Skunk: The Easy Rider

Kim opened her eyes early as usual that morning. Then quickly squeezed them shut, remembering what she had to do that day. "No, I'm not ready, you can't have her," she groaned, and fell back to sleep. Skunk, her border collie mix, snoozed at the foot of the bed.

Kim had been preparing herself, and Skunk, for this day for two weeks. She'd set a date and a time. Skunk at age 15 now labored to move her body, to carry out even the ordinary moments of everyday life as she had known it. The mild infirmities of old age had grown into full indignities.

For this dog especially, the indignities were frustrating. Skunk, after all, was a motorcycle babe. A horse trainer's sidekick, a free-spirited rider tooling across the countryside on the back of a chrome two-wheeler. As Kim rode the cycle from barn to barn training horses, Skunk was always onboard.

Riding High

Skunk had barked her way into Kim's life as an eight-week-old pup at the SPCA. "She never took her eyes off me from the minute I walked in; she just barked and barked," Kim recalls. "I wanted a golden retriever and had no intention of getting anything else. But my friend convinced me to take this border collie out of the cage. Black and white, like a skunk, she was probably the runt of the litter and likely had watched all of her littermates being taken. She was smart enough to know she'd better get somebody."

What she got was a young woman who made her living training horses and teaching humans how to handle them and understand equine behavior. A day in Kim's life meant traveling miles and miles from barn to barn through the green valleys of Pennsylvania's Chester County—on a motorcycle. "I didn't have a car for years," Kim says.

So Kim designed a seat on the motorcycle especially for Skunk. Every morning the dog would jump up, place her bottom and back feet on her special seat, her front paws on Kim's seat—and her nose on Kim's shoulder.

"When I was teaching her to ride the bike, Skunk liked to point her nose down at the road and that would put me off balance. So I taught her to press her nose right here"—Kim points to the back of her shoulder—"and stay there for balance. She could sit up nice and tall and the seat gave her good traction."

Off they went, making their rounds. "Skunk rode with me on the bike 365 days a year. It was always me, Skunk behind me in her little seat and my saddle strapped on the back of the sissy bar."

"Sometimes I'd have to leave her at one barn to go to another where a dog wouldn't be welcome. At the end of the day I'd stop by the first barn and pick her up and she'd always be there. But when we'd get back home, there would be messages on my phone from other barns, saying, 'You weren't scheduled to be here today, but Skunk was around.' So Skunk had set out all over the valley looking for me, knowing my route. But by the end of the day she was right back where I'd left her."

If Kim was on horseback, Skunk would trot by her side. If Kim was teaching students from the middle of the arena, Skunk followed her moves in instinctively correct spatial range.

Skunk followed voice commands flawlessly. "When I'd go anywhere on the bike and park it, at the mall or the gym for instance, I'd just tell her to lie down on the seat and 'stay.' She would stretch out over the bike seat—and stay. Or if I'd go out for dinner, she knew all the cooks and who in the kitchen would give her food."

Skunk at the Bank

But it was at the bank where Skunk drew full celebrity status. Wearing a festive scarf or a funky hat, Skunk would bike on through the drive-in window perched behind Kim. "In the winter, by the time I'd take off my gloves and my goggles and turn to put my deposit in the mechanical drawer, the bank window would be filled with faces of people looking out in amazement."

"Everywhere she went, Skunk engaged in life."

When Skunk's body was no longer able to live the way it wanted to, Kim decided what she had to do. "An animal in nature would have been gone by that point." Kim's sister, a veterinarian, arrived the morning of the appointed day with the euthanasia cocktail. "I wanted to meet the needs of my animal, Kim reflects. "I didn't want her to suffer in the name of meeting my needs."

The day proceeded with the rituals of burial. "I carried her body out to the back of my pickup truck. It was pouring rain. I went to my friend's home, where many of my friends had gathered to bury Skunk. We put the dog in the earth and little by little she disappeared as spadesful of dirt fell on her. The kids wrote her name in rocks on her grave. We planted a plant and watered it."

That was the easy part.

"I remember at the end of that long day," says Kim, "coming home and making food for myself in the kitchen. The worst grief was looking down for Skunk's eyes, which were always looking up at me. I had no idea this was a ritual we were engaged in for years, until she was gone and she was unable to meet my gaze."

Watching for the Butterflies

Mourning her loss some days later, Kim called an animal communicator friend to see if she had any sense of Skunk now. The friend answered, yes, in fact she did. "Skunk feels great. She feels like she's flying, and whatever she thinks of, she can do. She thinks it's really neat to feel she can fly."

And Skunk would be sending Kim a gift, her friend added. "It's a surprise. But be watching for the *butterflies*. Just be watching for the butterflies."

A week later Kim and a friend set out for a morning ride on horseback. Kim was flying to Atlanta later that day to work with some horses, but decided to squeeze in a short ride first. "I was on a horse I had ridden many a time. I knew his behavior. He was a very quiet, docile, complacent horse."

But on this day, shortly into the ride, the horse "just shot off from underneath me," says Kim. For no reason at all. He had never done it before. "I stayed on just by the skin of my teeth. I managed to collect my reins—and halt him. And at the moment I pulled him up, in that very spot, out of a bush beside us—rose a cloud of butterflies. All of a sudden they were everywhere. Light, small, flying up and all around. Lots and lots of butterflies."

Riding a short distance behind her, Kim's friend shouted out, "The butterflies—Kim, look at the butterflies!"

"It looked like a mass hatching," says Kim, "suddenly flying up out of this bush—exactly where the horse had abruptly stopped. I assume they had just been born, but I don't know."

Fitting for a Nature Girl

Grateful to have been brought to the burst of butterflies—and to have survived on a runaway horse—Kim caught her flight to Atlanta that day. She arrived at the horse farm, went through the main gate and on to the barn. Planters lined both sides of the barn entrance. Over them hovered—a host of butterflies.

"I have no idea what to make of the butterflies," Kim says. "But it was a fitting metaphor for Skunk's personality. She was a nature girl. A free, easy spirit. To this day when I see a butterfly, I think of Skunk."

"She gave me a great life."

The Dog Who Mourned at Ground Zero

"It doesn't look extraordinary at all," Liz Teal says. "It doesn't look as if anything is happening." Which is why she calls animal-assisted therapy and crisis response "invisible work."

But it has its extravagantly visible side too.

Visible in a dog highly trained, secure and comfortable in any environment. Visible in an owner or handler, careful not to push the dog too far in the acutely charged setting of trauma.

People and animals have long partnered in the work of the human day: Horses pulling plows, riding into battle, transporting humans and their cargo; dogs rescuing disaster victims, sniffing the scent of crime.

But now the pairing of human and animal has taken on more subtle work: comfort and connection in times of disaster.

As it did in the shatters of Ground Zero following September 11.

Working in New Territory

Immediately, canine units went to work with firefighters, police and rescue teams in recovery efforts—the dogs searching debris with keener-than-human senses.

Animal-assisted therapy came in later with the mental health support and spiritual care teams that followed those first responders. But in this setting, the dogs had a different role. It wasn't their noses or paws that counted here, but something invisible: their capacity to connect with survivors isolated by extreme grief.

The job of the dog-assisted therapy teams is to penetrate the complicated state of human suffering with the uncomplicated presence of an animal.

Liz Teal, an animal behavior consultant, specializes in animal-assisted therapy and crisis response. Annie, her dog and working partner, is a 12-pound toy spaniel. "Very pick-upable," by Liz's description. Which is not absolutely necessary for this work, but being a small, handlable package can ease the way.

And so it did on the ferries to Ground Zero.

"A lot of people who lost loved ones just needed to go down and see the site," says Liz. A few weeks after September 11, the Family Assistance Center arranged for families to do that—by boat. The ferries were small—the size of yellow school buses. On board were Coast Guard chaplains, state troopers and armed guards—as well as mental health support teams, including a canine crisis intervention team. The ferries set out from the 54th Street Pier on their short ride to Lower Manhattan, the World Trade Center site.

All the ferry passengers shared the common bond of loss and shock—but in hugely different ways. "You had people on these boats who knew their loved ones were dead. You had people who didn't know. You had people who were still thinking there were pockets down there that could support life. So the emotions on the ferries included a range of shock, grief and denial. All of that is very isolating," Liz says.

"Nothing comes close to what we witnessed and smelled there. Knowing a member of your family was part of that, this was the extreme of grief on board."

Once on the boat, passengers had a choice to make. Which side to stand on? The side looking back—to New Jersey, north and west; or the Manhattan side, facing south and east on the Hudson—toward Ground Zero.

A Slow Turn to the East

Liz and Annie's work started as soon as people saw the dog. "I would put Annie on the ground and we would walk the boat. And she'd just stop in front of someone. Often the person wasn't looking at Annie or me; they were looking north and west—to New Jersey. I would pick Annie up and the person would just reach over and start petting Annie. Then they'd grab her and hug her. And as they were holding her and petting her, they would slowly, slowly, start to turn and look—east. To the site." Until they could fully turn around and face the looming vestiges and vacancy of the Lower Manhattan skyline.

One woman with Annie in her arms did that. And as she turned fully to the devastation, she dropped the dog—into Liz's waiting arms. From there the woman walked over to family embraces.

Most times on those encounters, no words were ever exchanged.

"People would just come over and pick Annie up. These grave faces would go staggering toward the dog—to help them come out of shock," Liz says. "The dog was a safe thing to hold, to nurture."

"Animals are just *present*," says Liz. "We humans have a tendency to think in the past or the future. So in grief, the dog is an effective force in moving people back to the moment—where they can connect with the social group again."

"You have to recognize, of course, that there are going to be people on site who are scared of dogs. It doesn't matter how cute or effectively trained my dog is, if a person is afraid of dogs," Liz points out.

"That's why you never send your animal in until you as a handler have gotten eye contact or clearance from the person to make sure it's okay."

Except for that one time on the ferry when Annie saw otherwise.

"I'd Forgotten I Like Dogs"

"We had just finished working with somebody, so we sat down to regroup on one of the picnic-style benches and tables. I thought Annie would just climb into my lap and collapse because that's what she usually did."

Liz noticed a woman nearby completely absorbed in herself. "It's as if you could see a cement wall around her. She was sitting across from another woman in a very similar state. They weren't talking about anything. Maybe they would say three words, like, 'Nice peach blouse.' Literally, that kind of non-talk."

"As soon as we sat down, Annie shot right over to this woman, sat down by her and popped her with her paw. Tapped her on the thigh with her little paw."

"I said to the woman, 'I'm sorry. Her name is Annie. Annie, come back over here.'"

The woman looked up. "That's okay," she said. "I actually like dogs. I'd forgotten I like dogs."

Annie immediately lay down—putting her two paws and her head on the woman's thigh. The woman started petting the dog. And at the same time, the woman's other hand reached across the table to her friend. Her friend, without looking up, reached across the table and they held hands. The woman let go of Annie on her lap, reached over and took the woman's other hand. The two of them were looking into each other's faces with tears falling."

Annie crawled back over into Liz's lap. "Her work was done."

"A toy spaniel laps up to a person—no one would look at that as anything extraordinary," Liz points out, "but not just any dog can do this. The dog needs to have training and so does the owner or handler. You have to know what trauma and crisis look like; what people's different responses are. You have to know how to recognize your dog's needs, limits and particular stress signs, which can be subtle. Or even misleading. Maybe the dog gets a little more animated. Does more nudge-nudge, pet-me, pet-me. That's the training—knowing these stress signals," says Liz.

How does the dog choose whom to work with? "I don't know," says Liz. "I do know if you keep trying to direct the dog to whoever you think that person is, the dog burns out faster. There is a mutuality that has to be there."

The Circle Forms

As it was with the row of men.

In the first days after September 11, Liz went down to the site, looking to see how she and Annie might be of help. "I knew we were needed—but there was no protocol yet for how animal-assisted crisis response would work with the emergency management agencies."

Walking the blocks around the Armory, which was set up as a temporary Family Assistance Center, Liz and Annie scouted leads on how to provide support.

The scene was a panorama of posters. "Missing" posters. Everywhere, on billboards, telephone poles, tree trunks, on makeshift stands. Along with these were flowers, candles—and other posters advertising counseling groups.

Liz was writing down the number for one of the counseling groups she thought might use their help—when she noticed a line of men standing near the corner.

There were six of them. All in business suits, all immaculate. Dressed for the workday. But not going to any office that day. Each one stood a little bit farther from the next as the line stretched out a half-dozen suits long.

Annie sat down by one of the men, wagged her tail, and looked up. The man looked back at Annie. "Oh, God, I had a dog like that when I was a little kid," he said. He bent down and started petting her—and picked her up.

"The next thing I knew, Annie and I are in the center of what is by now a circle of these men. One of them is holding my dog. And they start, one by one, these isolated suits, making eye contact. One looks at the other one; they all start reaching out to Annie. They're all petting the dog."

Then one man looks up at another and says, "My wife."
The other one looks back and says, "My sister."
Another one, "My mother."
Suddenly these tailored suits are now men speaking their unspeakable sorrow to one another—facilitated by a small dog.

"I took Annie back and exited the circle. That was it. Our work was done there."

How Does Annie Do It?

Did Annie target that man in the line—choose him with a here's-who-we-need-to-work-with selectivity? Or did that set of human eyes find her first? "Couldn't tell you," says Liz. "But she does it consistently."

Is it the touch factor? "Might be," Liz considers. "When people are desensitized to human touch, they will often reach out more readily to an animal than another human."

Annie spots someone she needs to lap up to on the ferry. Annie is the fleshy bundle that grounds a grieving survivor enough to look at what has happened and accept human comfort. Annie the dog is the touchable, wordless center of a circle of men where eyes can begin to look into other eyes.

"That was Annie *doing* something."

"And it looks so ordinary," says Liz. "As if nothing extraordinary is happening at all."

The Soft Underbelly of Roo

The story of Kanga and Roo (complete with happy ending) began in a junkyard in a jagged neighborhood in North Philadelphia. Littered with abandoned trucks from the meat slaughter trade, the junkyard was ruled by a drug-addled squatter, Thomas, who lived in an old school bus at the back of the property. Sharing the premises were dogs, German shepherd mutts, a couple of dozen of them, along with several litters of puppies. All were trapped there, and prey for Thomas's raging rampages with a meat cleaver.

Local residents walking by the fenced-in junkyard let it all pass, feeling no call to act. Except for Peter and Ginny. Graduate students in social work at Temple University, they had just come here from Boston, determined to be deliberately urban and take part in making a better world where they were needed. This, they found, began sooner than expected.

When Peter and Ginny caught the full drama of the foraging, tortured dogs, they took it up. They saw the hulking, supersize, demented Thomas chasing the dogs with a meat cleaver. They saw the suffering; saw the hungry pack searching for food.

So the couple started feeding the dogs. But Thomas caught on quickly and began chasing Peter and Ginny with the meat cleaver. So they went underground. Furtively, they started throwing food over the fence to the dogs. But this, they saw, was just a holding pattern. It wouldn't solve the problem.

Nightly Rescue Trips

When a story appeared in the local newspaper about Molly, the beagle who, in flames herself, rushed into the burning building to rescue her eight puppies, Peter read with interest. What caught his attention was the man in the story. It was Bill Smith of Main Line Rescue. Main Line Rescue had found an adoptive home for the scarred and burned Molly. Well, Peter thought, if that's the kind of work that man does, maybe he can help us here.

For the next eight months, Bill Smith and Peter made stealthy trips to the junkyard at night, catching the dogs. By day, Peter would sometimes try to be friendly and talk to Thomas. That might work one day, but the next the man would turn wild again and, knife in hand, chase Peter. So dog by dog, in humane traps or just by hand, the team of Peter and Bill saved 23 adult dogs and four litters of puppies. "And we placed every one of them," Bill can say.

Among those dogs were Kanga and Roo. By Thomas's hands, Kanga had only three legs now. Both females, Kanga and Roo linked fates there in the junkyard, in an extraordinary bonding.

It went this way. While Thomas dragged Kanga squealing around the junkyard, Roo followed right behind, shadowing Kanga the whole time and barking at Thomas. "A few truck drivers in the area would tell us what they saw," says Bill. They saw that not only did Roo shadow Kanga when she was being stalked by Thomas, but in fact Roo also protected the three-legged Kanga under her belly. There, Kanga nestled in. She would lie or sit. Almost in a coma by the time Peter and Bill rescued her, Kanga came to them easily. Capturing the wary Roo wasn't so easy; it took a humane trap.

Kanga and Roo were taken to the University of Pennsylvania Veterinary Hospital. The medical team operated as they needed to on Kanga's wound, readying her for life on three legs.

Here, in the next stage of their journey, before moving on to caring homes, the pairing of Kanga and Roo deepened.

A Puzzle-fit

Bill boarded the two at a local veterinary hospital until he could find homes. He had used this particular hospital for years, but this time he found his canine boarders shunted all the way to the back in a hot, unused kennel. Except for Bill's daily visits and one attendant who shared her lunchtime pizza with the dogs, it was isolation for Kanga and Roo. And bewildering new surroundings.

Kanga and Roo kept up their puzzle-fit companioning. Roo would stand on her four legs, Kanga sitting underneath on her three. "They were so incredibly close," says Bill. "If you pulled Kanga out from under Roo, she'd go back underneath."

Just at that time, Bill had plans to do what he rarely has done since beginning rescue work: get away for a few days' vacation. When he came back, he was distressed at what he found. Kanga's wound was open and bleeding—from dragging herself on the concrete run.

"I took Kanga out of there that day," Bill says. "She needed medical attention so I took her to another vet clinic." The new vet's assessment: Kanga would be incontinent because her lower spine had been broken. Bill suspected as much, since her tail just hung. He took her to his house until he could find her a home.

Kanga's prognosis notwithstanding, the right owner came forward. A retired nurse living in Maryland would love to have Kanga, lifetime of diapers or not. So Bill and Kanga got in the car, Kanga off to a new life. "I thought maybe I could place Kanga and Roo together, but the nurse couldn't take both."

"When I took Kanga away from the kennel that day, Roo let out a blood-curdling scream. Kanga was screaming too. It was like ripping two monkeys apart. It was one of the most difficult things I've ever had to do."

That same day he took Kanga from the kennel, Bill went back to check on how Roo was doing. And that's when Roo started doing it: holding up her leg.

Roo wouldn't put that foot down. "I kept checking her foot pads to see if there was any injury, but there wasn't," says Bill. "I thought maybe there was something wrong with her hip. Maybe she slid after I took Roo away because she was thrashing around so much." Bill made an appointment with another vet. The vet found nothing. Nothing wrong with her hip, nothing wrong with her pads.

"Then I realized. It was the same leg Kanga was missing. The left back leg."

Roo, like Kanga, now walked on three legs.

Socializing Roo

Bill took Roo out and put her in a new boarding facility while he continued his search for a home. At the new kennel, Roo resumed walking on four legs. When she got up to walk at all. Terrified by her new surroundings, she cowered in the back of the kennel for months. Bill would take her out for walks. Once, in a major scare, she chewed through her leash and ran off over the hills. Bill thought, "After all this effort, she's lost. One more wild animal in Valley Forge Park. I'll never get her back. I didn't cry or anything. I just thought, it's over."

So where did Roo run? Back to her kennel. Highly territorial, she knew the way home and headed straight for it.

"Roo is much more feral than Kanga," says Bill. "She's extremely timid. If you walked over and touched her head, she would close her eyes and just hug the ground."

In those early days after Kanga left, Bill was still looking for a home for Roo. Behavioral training was recommended to help socialize her, making her more adoptable. So he enrolled Roo in dog training classes. Puppy classes, even though she was fully grown, because mentally she was still a puppy. Roo had never had a puppyhood. "I practically had to carry her to class," says Bill. "She'd sit in the corner and I'd have to pull her out. It was like starting a lawnmower. She'd walk around the room, sniff a little, and then run back in the corner."

Early in the puppy class the trainer pointed out Roo to the group, explaining why this "big galoot," as Bill fondly calls her, was here in the midst of all these puppies. "This dog came from a junkheap," the trainer offered, filling the group in on Roo's hardscrabble background.

At that point, all of the parents took a step back away from Roo. All the children took a step forward.

But the real Roo did finally emerge—a super-friendly social animal, fond of people, especially children, and dandy with other dogs. Over the weeks Roo became beloved by the children, one shy boy opening up expansively to her and wrapping his arms around her; another, bringing in weekly bags of treats.

Enough Is Enough

But the right home never appeared, and so Bill decided Roo would be his dog. "Enough is enough. I have to do the decent thing and just keep her," he decided. Which is how Bill has ended up with eight canine residents in his modest home.

But Roo, well, she's an absolute gem. "In fact, I test other dogs with her. If I'm fostering dogs whose temperament I'm not sure of, I let them out in the yard with Roo. I've done this with hundreds of dogs and not one of them has ever had a problem with Roo."

"I'd do pet therapy with her if she weren't so scared. She'll come right up and lick your face. But she's afraid of loud noises. If I drop the phone, for instance, she's gone. Underneath the table."

To this day Roo reflects what Kanga is experiencing, though the two are separated by many miles. "This summer, Kanga was having health problems. And just at that time Roo started thrashing around like a wild animal. She'd go off her food. She'd try to get away—try to jump over the fence. Then I talked to Kanga's owner and found out that Kanga had had pneumonia at that time."

"This is one reason I keep her," Bill says. "People will never understand her story. She's an incredible dog."

A Prince, a Horse and Maslow Too

Prince Charming, a white poodle pup, sat regally upright in the back seat of the car, looking straight ahead, as if being chauffeured. The car came to a stop and parked. The driver opened the rear door. Prince Charming, instantly spotting a car waiting across the street, bounded out, raced over to the other car and jumped in. There to begin a long reign with the queen of his dreams.

That queen of his dreams would be Maureen Hall, life-long friend of animals and professional animal coach. Maureen has been training dogs and horses for performance in movies, television, traveling shows, stage and commercials for 50 years now. She also has run an animal behavior clinic and hosted two radio talk shows, advising people with pet problems. Over the years, hundreds of dogs, cats and horses have come her way.

Prince Charming entered her life the way most of her animals did—the horses, the cats, and the eight dogs in the household when Prince arrived. Abandoned, stray or unwanted, for all of them, this was the last stop.

"Prince came from a man who worked with my husband," Maureen says. "The man mentioned that this beautiful poodle lived on his street and had no home. The dog played with the kids, met them when they came home from school and caught balls with them out in the street. The man was feeding the dog and let it sleep on his porch, but he was just snowed under at the time with family members who were out of work. So my husband said, 'I'm sure my wife will take it. Bring it in in the morning and I'll have my wife meet you here.'"

Maureen pulled up the next morning and parked a good 70 feet down the street from the car that chauffeured the poodle. "When the man opened the door, the dog just sailed out. He came running down the street, straight to my car and jumped right in like he'd known me forever."

First It Was the Bike

She'd long trained horses for show business, but Maureen had never coached a dog. Nor did she intend to. But then Prince showed up, highly perceptive and enormously self-controlled. "Extraordinary," the vet called him, noting the dog even had a rare capability to control his own heartbeat! That degree of self-discipline would make him easy to train. Prince Charming was clearly something exceptional.

That "something" went beyond innate skill. What Prince also had was a rare passion for performance.

"The dog showed me what it wanted to do," says Maureen. "He knew from the start that we were to be a team."

Maureen recalls, "It began one day when I was out in the carport where we kept a child's bicycle with training wheels. Prince was nosing around out there—trying like heck to figure out how he could get on that bike! He was struggling so hard. He'd get on backward, he'd try to get all four feet up on the seat, and then he'd fall off. I didn't say anything. I didn't move. Finally I couldn't stand it, so I went over and sat him down on the bike and showed him how to put two feet on the pedals and two feet on the handlebars." Prince was overjoyed.

A star was born. So was a dog trainer. Maureen refitted the bicycle with short pedals that Prince Charming could reach. Off they went, happily beginning their work together. Over the months Prince learned more than 50 tricks and was ready for the performance world. Maureen also taught him entertainment basics for stage life: how to take direction, stop at a certain spot, perform difficult tasks and do whatever else the script called for.

But those were just the rudiments of Prince's performance capabilities. What he also did was take on personas for the stage with ease and delight. He would eventually star in character parts using more than 30 costume changes. There he'd go, parading across a stage on his back legs, slow and dignified as Uncle Sam in a red-white-and-blue, custom-tailored sequined suit. Or swaggering as Cowboy Joe, wearing leather chaps and packing a six-shooter. Or twirling gracefully as a ballerina in his tutu. Whether he made his entrance riding on a pony, an elephant or his own hind legs, Prince was fastidious in his performance, following Maureen's directions, even her thoughts.

A Partnership Flourishes

It was to be a prosperous partnership, lasting nearly 17 years and more than 10,000 shows. Maureen and Prince Charming worked in television, commercials, circuses and stage shows in an extraordinarily close partnership. It was a high-performance act—but in fact it was no act. Prince rose to performance heights not through force or pressure, but through the relationship, communication and respect he and Maureen shared. Maureen guided Prince to use the skills he enjoyed and excelled in.

And Prince did love his work. Just as passionately, he loved his leader, Maureen. "Nothing else mattered to him but his work and me," Maureen says of their long years together. Prince Charming was loyal to her and no one else—not Maureen's husband, not their son. Serious, with no mind for nonsense, Prince had a firm idea of what constituted a good day. "He couldn't wait to go to work. He'd jump out of bed in the morning and run in and see where his bicycle was. If it was sitting in the carport, he'd be just kind of forlorn: 'Well, okay, it's one of those days,'—and he'd mope around."

"But if the bike wasn't there, he'd go out to the truck where we carried all the props for the shows. He'd jump up in the truck, and if the bike was there, he'd run and bounce around—like, 'Hurry up! Let's go! Let's go!'" And if Maureen would so much as touch the air crate used for jet travel, Prince would jump inside, ready to go.

"Other dogs want to play together, sniff around, go off. Prince never bothered with any of that. He didn't play. He worked. He put his heart into it and he didn't have time for foolishness."

This was a serious dog. Serious enough to refuse treats for training. When she began training Prince, Maureen was told by other trainers to teach the dog a trick and then give him a treat. Not Prince. He'd turn up his nose at the treat. "It was as if I had insulted him by offering a treat for his work," Maureen says.

Showtime was everything to Prince, and he demanded high standards not only of himself but of the other animals in the show too. Take King, a German shepherd who shared the stage tours with Prince. King had a talent for jumping—but also had a comic streak in him. "He was a clown," says Maureen. "He just had fun with it. So King would get out on stage and sometimes make a very slight mistake. Maybe not go right back to his seat after he'd jumped through hoops. It would be so tiny a mistake the audience would never know. But Prince would know." And after the performance, when Maureen took the animals behind the curtain, Prince would immediately jump on King, growling. "It was like Prince was saying, 'How dare you go out there and not do it right.' He was just scolding him—like 'you big oaf.'"

If Peppi Did It . . .

Peppi was already part of Maureen's household when Prince arrived. Peppi was a four-pound toy poodle and Maureen absolutely delighted in him. Unlike Prince, Peppi had plenty of time for foolishness. Every evening when Maureen gave out treats to each pet, Peppi would frolic with the morsel. Toss it, jump on it, roll on it, hide it under a pillow, then go back and check to make sure no one had taken it. A couple of hours later, he'd eat it.

Prince was disgusted with this juvenile display. "He'd have a look on his face," Maureen says, "like, 'Oh, no, not that stupid, silly stuff again. But, oookay.'" Prince, in his style, would very seriously eat his treat and be done with it.

Maureen saw just how complete was Prince's devotion to her when the playful Peppi died. Prince, so disdainful of Peppi's treat-play and rambunctious silliness, observed the gap now. A ritual Maureen had delighted in had gone silent.

That was when Prince stepped in. Immediately after Peppi's death, he began doing what he found so distasteful—playing with his treat, just as Peppi had done. Now Prince would toss it, pounce on it, hide it. And only later eat it.

Prince did this every day now, and for the rest of his life.

The way Maureen sees it, it was as if Prince decided, "Well, you really enjoyed the other one doing that. I guess somebody's got do this job. It's not a fun job. It's an awful job. But I'll do it because you like it."

Picking up behavior of a deceased household animal is not that common in Maureen's experience. She sees Prince's actions as motivated by a desire to please her rather than an affectionate remembrance of a departed household companion. Prince, after all, had never closely bonded with the other pets, or people. Just Maureen.

The Horse Who Backed Away

Maureen has been able to bring forth that larger-than-self behavior in her animals time after time.

So it was with El Hijo, the Andalusian stallion she trained and performed with for 30 years. They did circus work, traveling shows, parades. A breed trained for bullfights in Spain, Andalusians are fiercely protective of their riders. "I called him Horse, not his registered name of El Hijo, because he and I decided that there were a lot of four-legged things that called themselves horses—but *he* was the *real* horse."

Early in training, when Horse was about four years old, he showed that he knew more than how to be a horse.

"I kept a large goat at the time, and a drunk driver ran through the fence and hit him. We tried to save the goat and put him in a pen next to Horse. Horse was very jealous. He would get upset when I'd go in to the next pen to take care of the goat. It was like, 'You ought to be over here with me.'"

One morning that changed. "I went out to take care of the goat, and Horse, instead of coming forward to the stall door as usual, like, 'Get over here and take care of me and forget everybody else'—that day did something completely different. He backed away from me, as if to say, 'I don't need anything. I'm okay. You take care of that sick goat.'"

The goat died shortly after that.

"From that day on I could rely on Horse's behavior as a gauge of a sick animal's state. I could watch how Horse acted and know when I was going to lose one of my animals. This big, demanding stallion would back away—like, 'I'm okay. You go take care of that one.' I began to watch this and saw that what he did with the goat was not going to be a one-time thing."

Trading Places

That expansive behavior is natural to an animal, Maureen believes. What happened with her fluffy black-and-white, seven-pound dog named Cutie Pie, didn't surprise her either.

When Maureen took in this dog it was starved practically beyond saving. But Cutie eventually thrived and lived for sixteen years, sleeping each night on a pillow beside Maureen's head. When Cutie Pie was 14 years old, Bitsy joined the household. Another stray, Bitsy was a tiny, brown, shaggy dog that Maureen also restored to health. Cutie Pie and Bitsy became best of friends. Then after a few years Bitsy became feeble and ill.

That's when Cutie Pie did what she did.

"We got in bed one night and Cutie took up her regular spot on the pillow right by my head and Bitsy took up her regular spot at the foot of the bed," recalls Maureen.

"Suddenly Cutie raised her head. She just stared down to the foot of the bed at Bitsy for a moment. Then she got up (they were very good friends), walked down and just touched noses with Bitsy for a few seconds. Not a whimper or anything, just silent rubbing of noses. And with that Bitsy got up, came up and took over the pillow by my head. And Cutie took the spot at the foot of the bed, which she had never done in all her years with us."

"It was like, 'You're sick, you stay up there by her head. That's where you belong.' There was never any more discussion about it between them. The little dog lived maybe four months after that. Every single night, Bitsy would now have the spot on the pillow by my head and Cutie would sleep at the foot of the bed."

None of this animal behavior, whether it's a high performance show business act or generous behavior toward other animals, surprises Maureen.

"This is normal for animals. But most animals don't get the opportunity to express it. Or they're in a household where people really don't know how to get this behavior in their animals. They don't know how to stop jealousy or prevent it. Jealousy is insecurity; nothing else. It doesn't happen if there is a right relationship to the animal and you guide the animal, rather than force it, to learn either household rules or high-performance acts."

From Survival to High Performance

How do you guide this behavior? "You do it Maslow's way," she says. "I follow the Maslow triangle with all my animals."

Psychologist Abraham H. Maslow posited that humans are motivated by a hierarchy of needs progressing from basic physiological survival to self-actualization. Animals have the same needs, and Maureen honors those.

First she assures the animals of safety. This is particularly important for the strays she brings in. "Cutie Pie had been starved nearly to death. I put her in a safe place. Out of danger. All she had to do was rest and sleep and feel, for the first time in her life, safe. I provided food and water, though she could only handle a bite or two at a time. Then she'd have to sleep before taking another bite or two. So I met those needs. Plenty of fresh water, air, food."

The next need is for the animal to understand how to fit in socially. It's a matter of understanding "what the rules are around here."

"I go right up the triangle," Maureen says. After the animal is confident of safety, food, water, shelter, after it knows it belongs and how this family or group operates, Maureen sits back. She looks to the top of the hierarchy: the self-realization of the animal. "I do nothing but observe and see what that animal's talents are. I do that with every animal I have. Horse or dog or anything."

Take King, the German shepherd who worked with Prince Charming and loved to clown. King arrived with a history—and an obsession. King was about to be euthanized. His owner had been drafted for the military and had to leave the dog with his father. But the father couldn't keep King because the dog was an irrepressible jumper, constantly leaping the six-foot fence in the yard. "They couldn't figure out a way to keep him without chaining him all the time and they didn't want to do that. So I said bring him to me. They said, 'But this dog can jump just about anything.' I said, fine."

Maureen could not resist the temptation to encourage this dog to do what he enjoyed most: jumping. "Our friendship and trust grew steadily, probably because I offered him something no one else had. I loved to watch him jump and encouraged him to go higher and higher. He got up to 8 feet, 4 inches. It was pure heaven because instead of cussing him for jumping, someone was saying, 'Go for it.'"

"We all want our talent to be recognized. The animal wants to be recognized for what it's good at. So by following this Maslow pyramid, when I get up to the top I step back and see what they really like, enjoy and are good at. King wanted to be recognized for jumping. When he found a human who encouraged that, he was in dog heaven. He would do anything in the world for me. Because here was somebody who finally recognized him for what he was good at."

On every step of the climb up the triangle of training there is clear direction and unquestioned motivation on Maureen's part: she is the leader—but her leadership is established through love, nurturing and kindness.

Never is any animal of any species hit, shouted at, chased with rolled-up newspaper, squirted with water or told it's a bad dog or a stupid cat. The result is an animal that is "so impressed with you that it will do absolutely anything in the world to please you and to have the honor of working and living with you."

Using negativity is never an option. "It only puts the animal on the defensive. If you are on the defense, you are not in a learning frame of mind," Maureen has found.

The Spirit of It

It's a matter of spirit, too, and that is an unquestioned basic in Maureen's approach. "I fully believe in the spirituality of animals and that we must respect that." She points to her part Native American Choctaw roots and her parents' early recognition of her way with animals as having fostered that respect.

"When we were living in LA and I was about two years old, every dog in the neighborhood would escape to our house and come sit on the swing with me. My father said they all adore you and you seem to understand them. So when I was five, the family sold everything they had in California and moved to Missouri and bought 500 acres so I could have all the horses and dogs and cats I wanted."

Eventually Maureen's father decided that even this was not a wholehearted enough commitment. "He knew I liked movie animals and tricks and so he took me back to LA where I could get instruction and training."

Are the animal interactions Maureen has fostered amazing? She doesn't think so. "All these things are everyday life once the animal has respect for you as the leader. And that respect can't be bought or hit into them. You can't demand it. You have to earn it. You have to show them you're always on their side, always there to work with them."

"But I don't want to give the false impression that all you have to do is love animals and you will be able to do all of this," says Maureen. "I have spent thousands of hours taking private lessons from two mentors and thousands of hours in the classroom. I still study the behavior of animals every single day of my life and I hope to continue to do that for as long as I live."

She reflects, "Oh, I have a hundred such stories."

A Cry in the Night
–and That's Not All

"I go for concrete facts. X plus Y equals Z for me," says Joel Moyer. "Otherwise I don't believe it."

Joel Moyer describes himself as a man of more scientific than spiritual mind. Not surprising for a doctor of optometry. He finds the precision of eye work satisfying, his day filled with consultations on lasik surgery and the management of three eye surgery centers. The way people see things is his business.

But the business of Baxter in the night—no optical surgery could produce that kind of vision, and no mathematical formula could make its X and Y neatly add up to Z.

The night was August 7th, just a few weeks after Baxter died. Baxter the basset hound had been with Joel and Sara for 12 years and was one of those Velcro dogs. As a seven-week-old pup, he'd attached himself to Joel in El Paso, Texas. Joel had never intended bringing a pup home to Pennsylvania. But having maxed out on sightseeing and knowing he was ready to get a dog when he got home, Joel thought, well, why not just go look at the nearest basset hound breeder. "Of course you can't just go *look* at a puppy," he admits. "I had to get him, so we flew back to Philadelphia together."

It's a Team

Baxter enjoyed a long and happy life. Sara, Joel's wife, a counselor and animal behavior consultant, soon joined the team, making a joyful family bond. Later a companion basset hound, Scooter, would come along, adopted at age seven from a basset hound rescue organization. Then came the cat, Epidermis Nevus. Epi for short.

"Wherever we were, Baxter was. He followed us everywhere. If we were downstairs watching the evening news and Baxter fell asleep, when he woke up and found we'd gone to bed, he'd come up." Upstairs to his blue comforter at the foot of the bed, where he slept every night, alongside Scooter, for 12 years.

He loved his people, Baxter did. "He was very well trained," Sara says, "but if you left for five minutes, when you got back he'd yowl like he hadn't seen you in 20 years. He gave you such a welcoming!"

Licking with Care

Even people who didn't like dogs liked Baxter. That's what made him a celebrity in his weekly pet therapy visits to the local hospital. "Everyone knew him," says Sara. "Patients who had been in the hospital and had to come back a couple of years later would ask, 'When is Baxter coming in?' The hospital staff looked forward to Baxter's Friday visits." So did Maggie, the resident rabbit, who would happily let Baxter lick her.

At home, the cat, Epi, fit right into the two-dog household when she arrived as a kitten. Scooter was accepting, if a bit bored with the whole cat thing. But Epi and Baxter—now *there* was a bond. They enjoyed instant affinity. Baxter welcomed the kitten with a practice that became a ritual.

"Every night after dinner, Baxter would lick the cat," Joel recalls. "Not just a little—he would lick her soaking wet." For Epi, who is hairless, that meant a total skin drenching. A calico sphinx, her breed has a suede-like, peach-fuzz coating. "The cat would let Baxter lick her to a certain point. Then, it was enough," says Joel. "She'd swat at him and he'd stop. But a little later she'd want him to do it again, so she'd walk up and rub her back against his face and he'd start again." They would perform the ritual every night.

That practice became a barometer of Baxter's health. "When Baxter was sick that last month, he stopped licking Epi," says Joel. "Even if she got close to him, he would turn his head away. When we'd put him on different medications, sometimes he'd start licking the cat and we'd say, 'Look, he's doing better! He's licking the cat!'"

But when Baxter could not walk, when he was in too much pain to be carried in or out, he was lovingly euthanized. It was July 13th.

Only a week before, Sara and Joel had taken Baxter to a small courtyard shopping center for a brief outing because Baxter loved to see people. In his usual mode he would be wagging his way forward greeting people, but now Baxter could only lie quietly, too weak to respond. Getting up to go, Sara and Joel started walking toward the car—when Baxter spotted a very young woman in a wheelchair. Their eyes met, the woman reached out with, "Oh a basset hound," and Baxter, who until then had nothing left to offer, went over and licked her.

Deepening the loss for the Moyers, Scooter had died only two months before.

At the Bedroom Door

The house was quiet without Scooter and Baxter. Some things changed. Some didn't. For years the Moyers had slept with the dogs at the foot of the bed. The bedroom door would be closed, because if it were open the dogs would occasionally go downstairs and make a bathroom out of the dining room rug—rather than wake up the humans to be let out.

In summertime, closing the bedroom door kept the air conditioning and the dogs in. But it kept Epi out. That was fine with her, given how chilly that bedroom felt to a hairless cat. It was better upstairs in the attic, with its delightful desert-like heat. There a bare-skin cat could keep cozily warm all night.

After the dogs died, Epi for the first time ever would cry to get into the bedroom. Joel and Sara started leaving the door open a crack for her. Once she remembered how cold it was in there, she walked right out. Back to the attic.

"But once in a while we'd forget and close the door all the way," Joel says. "Then we'd hear Epi crying to get in, and I'd remember, 'Oh, that's right, the door's shut' and I'd open it. She'd feel how cold it was, and walk away."

"What happened on this particular night, August 7, was strange," Joel tells. "It was about three or four in the morning, and I heard Epi crying. Just her typical cat meow, nothing out of the ordinary. I'm a light sleeper and woke up—my side of the bed is right near the door—and I looked to see if the door was shut and was going to get up and open it. But I noticed it was already open. And Epi was not there. I thought, that's kind of weird. So I tried to go back to sleep."

"Then Epi started crying more. But the cry changed. She made a sound we'd never heard from her before and haven't heard since. It was like a baby crying. Very, very loud. Epi is only about seven pounds, so she doesn't have a big voice. The cry was somewhere between a happy sound and pain. It would make you uneasy."

"I started to get concerned," Joel remembers. "I thought maybe she was hurt or sick or caught behind something. So I was about to get up and see if she was okay. But when I looked through the crack in the doorway, I saw Epi was sitting right there."

"Then I saw Baxter coming through the doorway."

Movement and a Silhouette

"When I looked at the doorway, I saw movement, a transparent gray dog silhouette. It was half in and half out of the door when I first saw it. He moved at his normal gait, tail wagging, to the end of the bed and disappeared into the darkness."

"His whole body was one coloration—a see-through gray. But it didn't blend with the dark. It was outlined. You could see it was totally separate. He didn't appear as a shadow. All I could see was the top of his head, his ears, his back and his tail. Then I saw his hindquarters walking with his tail wagging toward the foot of the bed."

"He didn't look at me. I didn't see his face. He just walked right past Epi through the door into our bedroom past the bed on my side with his tail wagging."

Joel's reaction? "It totally freaked me out. I closed my eyes. My heart was racing at this point. And when I opened my eyes again, Epi was gone and so was Baxter. I was like, 'What just happened?'"

Why Baxter and not Scooter? "I don't know," says Joel, "but I know it was Baxter." The shape, the walk, the wagging tail, all distinctly Baxter. Baxter was svelte for a basset. Trimmer, with a thinner tail, legs and arms than Scooter.

"If it's a person you know, even a shadow of someone you know, you can say, for instance, 'Oh, that's Sara,'" Joel says. "The way he looked, even though it was all gray, it was enough to say, without a doubt, that was Baxter."

There was no attempt to communicate on Baxter's part. Instead, his movement, Joel describes, was more like, "Oh, I'm going to lie down at the foot of the bed to be with you like I usually am."

"The weirdest thing is that as soon as I opened my eyes and saw Epi in the doorway, she stopped crying. That's when I saw Baxter walk in. It was almost like Epi cried to let me know Baxter's here. As soon as I opened my eyes, I saw him walk by. And that was it. It was very quick."

Sara woke up and asked, "What's the matter?" Epi had been making some noise, Joel told her. "Oh I thought I heard that," Sara said. "And that's not all," Joel added.

Walking On

A sleepy vision, a half-awake dream? The trouble with that is that Joel was fully awake, and in another second was going to get up to see why the cat was crying that eerie sound.

What was the feel of Baxter in that walk-by visit? Did Joel get the sense that Baxter was happy? "I did," Joel reflects. "When he didn't feel well, like in the last month of his life, his tail was down. But we were lucky. Most of his life he was a healthy dog. His tail was always up and wagging, in the way of a dog who's excited. That's the way I saw him every day. And that's how it was when he walked by me that night."

"In fact, if I had to put my finger on it, it was actually the tail—straight up—that made me think he was okay and happy."

For days afterward Sara woke up asking Joel, "Did you see him last night?" "No, I didn't," Joel would laugh—and be on with the day.

Baxter, apparently, had walked on.

Is That You, Malibu?

One thing puzzled the vet during Malibu's last visit. "What confused him," Robyn recalls, "was that when a dog is ready to die, its spirit is gone. But Malibu's eyes were bright. She'd lift her head and look around, still curious. Her spirit had a kick to it. You could see it."

It was always the eyes that connected Malibu with Robyn. In the dog's eyes a bubbly spirit flashed, even when she was sitting and waiting patiently for Robyn to say, "Malibu, want to go out?" Leaping with excitement at the prospect of a walk, Malibu would jump up, twirl around, wag her whole body back and forth. "She was full of joy and fun," says Robyn. "So excited to do everything she did."

That Malibu zest, the jump of grateful joy, the sparkle in the eye, is what brought Robyn and Malibu together some six years before. They met on the road. In a red Miata, Robyn had set out from home in Pennsylvania on a cross-country odyssey after a deep loss in her life. By the time she reached California, Robyn felt a powerful urge: to have a dog. Not one to put things off, she headed for the nearest animal shelter. It was in Malibu.

A Lap of Her Own

At the shelter the expected aggregation of dogs greeted Robyn, all vying for attention and a chance to get out. Among them was a lhasa apso terrier mix with long, golden-tan hair and black eyes peeking through a floppy mane. The dog went directly over to Robyn and sat down beside her. It was a match, right there.

All the way back across the country, Malibu draped herself across Robyn's lap, quickly claiming her place as the dog of Robyn's life.

Once back home in Pennsylvania, it was Robyn, her husband Ed and Malibu side by side. A few years later they all logged 2000 miles together across the country when Robyn and Ed moved their lives west to the Rocky Mountains. It was a new settling-in, for the people, the dog—and the cat, Whip.

But a couple of years later Malibu's health deteriorated. It was kidney failure, progressive and irreversible. Intensive IV treatment could not stem her rapid decline. Malibu was now restless, unable to get comfortable in any position.

On the living room floor late on a February night, seeing the coming close of life for her dog, Robyn wanted to build a comforting fire for both of them. With no wood at hand, she made do with a candelabrum shaped in an arc of seven rainbow colors. Sitting long and late, Robyn watched with Malibu until one by one each candle in the spectrum went out. Robyn carried Malibu into the bedroom, hoping the dog would settle down there. But Malibu was up and down on the bed, finding no peaceful rest. Robyn helped her to the floor. If Malibu made it to the morning, Robyn and Ed would take her in for euthanasia.

Whip Watches

Throughout the night Robyn sat at Malibu's head, with Ed at Malibu's back. Malibu would lift her head. "She was scared," Robyn remembers. "It was in her eyes—the look of fear. I was telling her, 'It's okay, Malibu. Peace.' And she lay her head down, but she was afraid."

When her last breath came, Malibu's tail went flat. Her head settled to the floor. It was four in the morning.

At that moment Robyn heard a noise. Whip, the cat, had hopped up on the bed.

"Understand, Whip almost never came into the bedroom," says Ed. That was Malibu territory. "In two years maybe the cat had been in there a few times." As housemates, Malibu and Whip were always together—but hardly best friends. "They pretty much ignored each other," says Ed. Except when Malibu would amuse herself by chasing Whip.

Black, round and plump, Whip rarely roused herself. This was not a cat tempted by adventure. Whip's notion of a vigorous day's work would be opening her eyes in half-looks and lazily meandering over to the food bowl. Being of so serene a nature, she coexisted placidly with Malibu.

But in Malibu's parting moments, Whip zoned into a high-pitched state of alertness. "Perched on the edge of the bed, she hung her head over, wide-eyed at what was going on with Malibu," Ed recalls.

Like Malibu, Like Whip

The next day carried all the emptiness of a home recently absent a beloved family member. But it was Robyn and Ed's high season in the ski resort of

Breckenridge, Colorado, where just a few months before they had opened a coffee-and-ice-cream café. Work called and they went.

But, deeply pained, Robyn and Ed cut short the workday and came home mid-afternoon. Bracing herself for seeing the empty spot at the top of the stairs where Malibu had always waited, Robyn opened the door and looked up. There sat Whip.

When Robyn reached the top of the stairs, Whip rolled over for a belly scratch. Just as Malibu had always done.

Together Robyn and Ed sat by the sliding glass doors that afternoon, looking out on their mountain and lake view, laughing and crying, talking about Malibu. "It was such an empty time," Robyn says.

Then they noticed something. Rainbows. Surrounding them, reflected from a crystal prism hanging in the window. Rainbows on the wall beside them, on the facing wall, above the sliding glass doors, on the metal door handle. "Rainbows everywhere, surrounding us," Robyn recalls.

Though they'd sat there, same time, same place, same sun for two years, "It had never happened before and it's never happened since," says Ed.

The next morning, Robyn and Ed followed the habits that always began their fast-paced day. But first they took their usual quiet time together on the sofa by the window overlooking the Rockies. Malibu would always be in the middle.

"As soon as we sat down that morning, who came to sit between us but that cat. Head on my lap." Just like . . . well. Everything that Malibu did, Whip now did.

Two days after Malibu died, the mystery deepened. Malibu had a nightly habit of pawing open the cabinets on the kitchen floor, foraging for snacks from her food supply. Robyn would come out in the morning to find the cabinet doors ajar. "Malibu loved to eat," says Robyn.

"I got up that morning two days after Malibu died, came out to the kitchen—and all the cabinets on the floor were wide open. Every cabinet."

It was early, about six a.m. To check that she wasn't dreaming or hallucinating, she went and shook Ed awake. "Come look at this," she said, wanting someone else to witness the cabinets, all opened, shades of Malibu.

Whip kept it up. Rolling on her back, cozying up to Robyn and Ed, claiming the sitting space between them, putting her head on Robyn's knee, Whip continued to do what the dog had done. Wherever Malibu would have been, Whip now was.

Moving On

The third day after Malibu's death, Robyn came home to find Whip, again, sitting at the top of the stairs just like Malibu. "This was too weird," Robyn decided. "Whatever was happening here, it was time for it to stop." So with irony or not, Robyn said to Whip, "Malibu, are you in there? Malibu, I love you and I'd love you to stay, but you died. You need to go now. You need to move on.'"

For whatever reasons Malibu's habits or presence had lingered, the time had now passed.

Not at that moment, but the next day, the cat was the cat again. Settled, serene, composed on the chair in her usual way. Curled. Quiet. Pure Whip.

Glimpse of a Ghost

Sixty feet beneath the waves, Joan was sitting in a funk.

Joan deep at the bottom of the sea was nothing new. An experienced scuba diver, she had been down there dozens of times before. She'd played with the fish, poked at the plants, delighted in every unexpected sight. And this wasn't just any underwater world. This was Hawaii, one of the most lavish fish bowls on earth. A scuba diver's dream.

Even so, Joan was in no mood to explore the colorful undersea life surrounding her. Not just days after what happened with Shelby, her dog. In fact, Joan didn't want to be here at all. Didn't want to be in Hawaii. Didn't want to be scuba diving. Didn't want to be anywhere.

Now, years later, Joan still can't account for what happened that day. Maybe it was imagination. But after it happened, all in a moment, Joan's grief lifted. Her outlook permanently changed.

Home for Joan was Pennsylvania, where she and her brother—and Shelby—shared a house owned by her mother.

A springer spaniel, Shelby was the dog Joan had always wanted. "My whole life I wanted a springer spaniel but I waited until I could take on the responsibility," she says. With a new job in retailing now, Joan finally knew what her schedule would be. She could reliably come home at the end of the day and fit a dog into her life. "So I got her. My daily excitement would be to come home and take Shelby rollerblading. We went out together every night after work. I'd skate and she'd run along beside me."

Life being good, a boyfriend enters the picture. The kind who wants to take you to Hawaii for a vacation. Family being close, Mom stops by the day before Joan and her boyfriend are to leave. To say hello to all, Shelby especially. And to make some of her famous chocolate chip cookies.

The Lure of Chocolate

"Shelby loved when my mom cooked. She knew if Mom was in the kitchen she'd get nibbles of something good. She'd stand by the counter and bark for a treat." That day as usual Shelby got a sample of dough—without the chocolate chips, which are especially unhealthy for dogs. But Mom finds she is short of chocolate chips. Only half a bag, when it takes a full bag to turn out the kind of cookies that had earned her a reputation.

So in the middle of cookie making, not yet adding the half-bag of chocolate chips to the dough, Mom decided to make a quick trip to the store for more chocolate.

"When my mother got back," Joan tells the story, "my brother was standing over Shelby who was lying on the living room floor." He'd given the dog mouth-to-mouth resuscitation. But it was too late. Shelby was gone. "When I got home from work I saw my mother and brother standing at the door. I knew something was wrong. Mom was crying. 'We're sorry. We don't know what happened.'"

What happened? The evidence was an empty half-bag of chocolate chips on the kitchen floor. As best the vet can put together the scenario, Shelby got into the chocolate chips on the kitchen counter, gorged herself and suffered a heart attack. The cocoa and caffeine in chocolate, particularly baking chocolate, can speed up the heart rate of dogs to fatal levels. Even in frisky three-year olds like Shelby. Death by chocolate.

"I could not understand it. She was running around like crazy before all this. I was heartbroken. She was my baby."

To Go or Not to Go

Tomorrow was the Hawaii trip. Impossible, Joan cried. "I was *not* going to go to Hawaii. I felt like I was going to have a nervous breakdown. But my boyfriend kept pushing me to go. I didn't want to. I cried the whole time. I'm even afraid to fly and thought the plane was going to crash. But I was so heartbroken I didn't care."

Fine start for a blossoming romance. "I couldn't sleep at night I was so unhappy. Who knew if our relationship was even going to last after this?"

But both Joan and her boyfriend were scuba divers. That was partly the purpose of the trip. "It took everything in my power to get up that morning and go scuba diving. I was crying every twenty minutes."

Joan got herself to submerge that day, even in her overwhelming grief. "It wasn't like me to have no heart for this. I'm an avid scuba diver. But I was so unhappy I just didn't want to be there. I didn't want to be anywhere. All I could think about was my dog. How much I'd miss her. And what was I doing in Hawaii at a time like this when I should be home mourning Shelby?"

But, weighted with a belt, Joan descended and sat on the bottom of the ocean. Just sat. Undulating with the waves, she drifted back and forth with the tidal rhythms.

"Then, in the distance, maybe fifty feet away, I saw her. I saw Shelby swimming by."

Swimming with the Currents

"She was swimming like a mermaid. She wasn't coming toward me; she wasn't playing with me. She didn't look at me. And I didn't try to touch her. I just sat there. Just then, a stream of calmness came to me and in it were her words. 'I'm okay, Mom. I'm going to be fine. I'm happy.'"

"Some type of warmth shot through me. It lasted maybe five seconds—with Shelby's words going through me, telling me she's okay and it's time to go on with your life and be happy. It was an instant, so brief, but it changed my mood permanently. A huge calm came over me."

"Then she passed out of my sight. She did not look at me. I just saw her swimming, undulating up and down with the current of the waves and the water."

"It kind of scared me. But it was the most calming, soothing thing that ever happened to me. In that instant Shelby made it easy for me to come out of grieving. Such a warm calming feeling came over me."

Joan, at that point, looked around for her boyfriend (who later became her husband—yes, it worked out) and the two shot up to the surface together. "I came up and said to him, 'You're not going to believe what happened down there.'" She told him the story. "Yeah, whatever," he said. "But I'm glad you're happier."

"That's what it was like," Joan tells. "I was a whole new person after that. I could talk about Shelby. I could recall the fun things we did together. I didn't even go back later to look for her down there because I was so calm. Everything was fine."

Shelby's intention was not to come to her, Joan believes. Rather it was to have Joan see her. "She was doing this to make me feel okay. She was comforting me. I just looked at her and couldn't believe it. I thought it was my imagination—but I wasn't even thinking about imagination. I just accepted that this was happening and she was doing this to make me feel okay."

"From that day, it was okay. Since then, I've never had an unhappy feeling about Shelby."

Being Scruffy

From the start, this scrappy black-and-white kitten showed the feisty stuff to take over a family of four.

And Scruffy he was in those early days. Born in a large litter at a stable, all but one of his siblings run over by the train, killed by a bulldog or kicked by horses, he knew he had to get out. So when he saw Brian, Joy and their two young boys, Brian and Brendan, walk into the barn to choose between the two remaining kittens, Scruffy leaped—right into the pocket of Brian's sweatshirt.

"Before he accepted us, of course, he wanted to see the family balance sheet, last year's tax return, what kind of accommodations we offered," Brian laughs.

Scruffy had bagged the home cat dreams are made of. Brothers to play with! Brian and Brendan, third and fifth graders then, were his eager companions. People all day! The McGowan CPA practice was home-based, so Scruffy could hang out with Brian and Joy in the office and, when clients came in, get fussed over.

Come three o'clock, when it was time to stretch and look for the boys to get home from school, there were games to play! Out to the backyard for football, sprinting back and forth across the field. For basketball, Scruffy would have to devise intervention strategies to get the attention he deserved. Saunter on to the court, flop down under the hoop and, to shouts of, "Come on, Scruff, move!"—stop the game cold. Worked every time.

"He thought he was one of the kids," says Brian.

After dinner, curl up on the kitchen table where Brendan did his homework from six to nine every night, all through elementary and high school. Then it was upstairs for family TV. And a mother who doted—Joy, the caregiver, the one you could wake up every night to let you out and who waited up until you felt like coming back in. What fun—watching her calling "Scruffy" there in the doorway in her pajamas to no response—until she shook the box of cat treats—then you'd come flying. And in later years, you could jump up on the bed and meow to get her to walk you down to the basement litter box, three times a night if you felt like it, because you wanted company.

Guarding the Fiefdom

There were duties involved, of course. "The backyard was his fiefdom," Brian says. "His job in life was to take care of it. You had bushes that had to be peed on, squirrels that got in the way. You had birds, rabbits."

And that old opossum that jumped on Scruffy and rolled him on his back, only to have Scruffy leverage the power of his back legs and send the critter spinning into the bushes. "All the animal intruders had to be instructed that this was Scruffy's block," says Brian. "Scruffy let them know if they behaved, they could stay. But it was a lot of work, managing the territory."

Oh the games they played! "Cats have different relationships with different people," as Brian sees it. "They know they can do certain things with certain people. They know who the feeder is. That's easy to figure out."

And young Brian, Scruffy deduced, was the game person.

It started when Brian was wrapping Christmas presents. Scruffy, mesmerized by the ribbon, launched an attack. Smacked the ribbon, rolled on his back and batted it some more. Loved the game. So when young Brian put the ribbon back in the apothecary chest by the front door, Scruffy caught on. Every day before breakfast, Scruffy would sit by the chest or turn his head that way, signaling for young Brian to follow him. "I'd get the ribbon out, he would cry out in excitement and we'd play. That went on for 10 to 12 years."

And how many cats know how to play baseball? Discovering that game, too, was pure serendipity. Young Brian, doing homework one night, crumpled up a piece of paper and threw it away. "But I missed the trash can and the ball of paper went down the steps. Scruffy happened to be at the bottom—and he swatted it a couple of times. So I figured I'll try and play baseball with him. I would stand at the top of the stairs, he would be below, and I'd throw crumpled paper in the air and he'd stand on his hind legs and hit it. Depending on what kind of whack it was, we'd say, 'Hey, Scruffy, that was a single, or that was a double.'"

Certain efforts to communicate with the family were more complex. Getting them to put that cushy soft jacket on the chair, for instance. "There were leather chairs in my dad's office, but they were uncomfortable for Scruffy," young Brian says. "Too hard. Scruffy liked fabric. One time Dad must have left his down jacket there, and Scruffy settled in and loved it. When he saw my mom putting it away, he must have followed her back to the closet."

The ritual began. "If Scruffy wanted to sit on that chair, he'd start screaming at the top of his lungs, so you'd follow him to see what he wanted," says young

Brian. He'd walk down the hallway to the closet and start pawing against the door. He wanted the winter jacket. Then he'd follow you back to the leather chair and you'd have to make a little bed out of the jacket for him, inside out, then he would hop up."

"Scruffy was a master of communicating," Joy observes.

Scruffy Finds Gold

Take the Christmas box, for example. "Joy has a neat collection of Christmas balls, all wrapped in soft tissue," Brian tells. "One day before Christmas she took the balls out and put the box with the tissue paper in front of the fireplace. Scruffy took a look at it and thought he'd found gold. The cardboard box, the cracking heat of the fireplace, the crunched-up paper. You couldn't get him out of the box. He would literally spend 30 days there from December 15 until we took the tree down a month later," Brian recalls.

"Strike me dead if I'm lying, but he knew when Christmas was coming. About two weeks before Christmas, he'd go to the attic door because he knew that's where we kept the box. It's almost like he was reading his little cat calendar; you know, '10 days 'til Christmas.' He did that for years."

Even so, the switch from the Christmas box to the fuzzy green basket was easy. "Just two years before he died, we got him this little green basket with a plug-in heater. He was in the Christmas box when we were opening our presents one Christmas morning. We said, 'Scruffy, here's one for you.' We put it right beside the Christmas box—and it was like he'd found gold again. He got out of the Christmas box—didn't even put a paw to the floor—and stepped right into the green one. He sniffed it, circled round and round, put his butt down and he never went back to the Christmas box."

The years pass. The boys grow up—but never outgrow Scruffy.

The boys-to-men join the family CPA practice. It's McGowan and Company now, including CPAs Brian, Brian, Jr. and Brendan, with Joy managing the office. The home base is no longer big enough to accommodate the expanded staff, so the McGowans renovate a home in the business district of town and turn it into company headquarters.

Scruffy comes to work every day. Joy and Brian pack him in the car and at the office, Scruffy goes right to his desk. Brendan's desk it is, under the lamp where it's warm, in his padded green basket. Curl, snooze. Around noon, catch the whiff of food. It's Joy in the kitchen getting lunch. He heads downstairs for nibbles. After lunch, it's back upstairs to his desk for the afternoon, until Joy gathers him up for the ride home.

So when it was time, how would Scruffy, at age 19, take his leave of this enchanted circle of family life?

Leaving the Circle

"We knew there was something wrong just a month after Christmas. He was lethargic, and we caught on that maybe it had to do with the electrical heat in the green pad. We figured it was like sitting in a hot tub all day. Your muscles just go limp. The doctors said no, it was his kidneys. The creatanine levels were really bad and maybe he had a month or two," Brian recalls.

But one beautiful April day, Scruffy sniffed spring in the air, got up from his bed—and went outside. "We had a respite there for a couple of years. But he was never quite the same. He slept 20 hours a day." Until then, Scruffy still had wild inside.

Up to a month before Scruffy died he was still going out, padding up and down the steps at the office four to five times a day. Which was not easy. "He tried to walk, he was so stubborn, but when he'd walk he'd collapse," recalls Brendan. "His paws would just fold under him. But he'd walk anyway on his folded paws."

He stopped eating. He stopped drinking. The McGowans took him to the vet, who gave him fluids for hydration. "We were hoping for a miracle," says Brian.

Rising Up, Reaching Out

Was it time? "Well, the little bugger looked at the vet, he hated going to the vet, and stood up, screamed, shook, and the vet said, 'Take him home, watch him and do what you're doing and we'll wait and see.'"

The McGowans took him home that night and to the office the next day. Two days later, on Friday, Scruffy lay in his green basket on Brendan's desk. "You couldn't get any movement out of him whatsoever," Brendan says. "You'd pick him up and his body was lifeless. You had to lift his head up. Before this he'd prop his head up on the rim of the green basket so he could look at you and see what's going on. This day he was lying flat and completely limp with a blank stare."

"We had all pretty much decided that day to call the vet for euthanasia. It wasn't fair to Scruffy. He hadn't eaten for eight or nine days and had stopped drinking for a week."

But what happened was strange.

"I guess it was four o'clock," recalls Brendan. "My Mom had just called the vet maybe five minutes before. He was going to meet us at the house at six. So Brian and I were spending time with Scruffy. He must have known we were upset."

Maybe that's why he did what he did.

"He was curled up in his green basket and Brian and I were sitting there talking to him and petting him. Then all of a sudden, after being limp for eight hours, Scruffy picked up his head, shifted his body, stood up on his paws, tilted his head and looked right at us. He put his left paw out to touch us. Then he lay back down."

"Brian and I said, 'Did you see that?'"

Young Brian recalls the moment. "He stood up, tilted his head almost 90 degrees to the left and his eyes went wide open and—it was like a giant smile on his face. He just stared at us both for maybe five seconds, then he relaxed back. God knows how he did it because he hadn't had any food in his system for days."

"All the way home in the car. I held him in the basket," Brendan remembers. "He was starting to make weird sighing noises like a baby cry. So we wanted to rush home to make him a fire. For the last two weeks we'd gone to our parents' house after work and sat with him in front of the fire for two or three hours." This would be the last fire.

"On the whole ride home his paw was curling around my hand and my finger. Which was strange because he had no hand flexibility before. No function in his muscles."

At home in front of the fire, all sat there, petting him.

During that last hour before the vet arrived, Scruffy reached out and kept looking around at the family. "At the same time was gripping our fingers with his paw," Brian says. Before that he'd been nearly comatose. "To me it was clearly a high level of communication," Brian believes. "He knew."

It's Cool, Folks

The vet arrived. He shaved Scruffy's paw.

"Scruffy looked at everybody once, as if to say, 'It's cool,'" Brian recalls. "I think he was saying, 'I've gotta move on. Hey guys, I had a great life and I'm going. And don't worry. It's okay.'"

"Somehow he got his head up in that basket and said goodbye to everybody," Brendan remembers. "Just looking at us like that made it a little easier for Brian and me."

Which, if Scruffy communicated it right—and when didn't he?—may be just what he intended.

How to Fetch a Human

When Callie found him, Herb was nearly 80 years old. Herb had waited a long time to be fetched by this dog; ever since he was a kid, in fact.

Not that Herb didn't have a dog when he was growing up. The family had a series of dogs, but each one seemed to have a knack for getting lost. Herb surmised that his mother was probably abetting these wanderings, but what's a boy to do. Never resentful, he still never stopped wanting a dog.

Later, when Herb married Miriam they had a daughter named Bonnie, and bought a house on Long Island. Now the time was right for a dog, and the family adopted a canine friend. But, not so fast there, Bonnie was allergic. It didn't work out.

When Bonnie grew up and moved away, Herb figured the prospects for getting a dog were never better. Why not a dog now? Miriam, not eager to have the disruption of a dog in the house, could think of several reasons. She pointed out the advantages of *not* having a pet at this later point in life. Easy travel. Freedom. And so forth. So Herb didn't make a case over it. But he continued to want a dog. Now, though, he would lay out the terms. Herb's proposition was this: "The dog will have to find me."

He and Miriam laughed lightly about it, and Miriam breathed easy, confident that no dog had "find Herb" on its list of things to do.

A New Way Home

On a May afternoon, Herb and Miriam were on their way home from the cardiologist. Herb had undergone quadruple bypass surgery several years before and at this point wasn't feeling well. The doctor acknowledged, "You're living on pills, Herb, and they're keeping you alive but, yes, they make you tired."

A melancholy was inching in on Herb, as he realized he hadn't the energy to do what he wanted to do. A trip into New York City? That was too exhausting. "Well, at least get out and walk," the doctor advised. Herb knew he should but somehow just didn't do it. This visit to the cardiologist offered no nostrums, no heartening promise of more vigorous health.

Herb's usual road home was down Hardy Street. But today he went a different route, taking a turn a couple of blocks farther away. Driving slowly, window open on this warm afternoon, Herb saw the dog just in time. A small brown-and-tan mix of a dog ran in front of the car. Herb braked.

Unharmed, the dog trotted around to Herb's side of the car, lifted its paws up on the window ledge, and gazed directly at Herb with dark brown, liquid, inescapable eyes.

Callie had found Herb. But she hadn't clinched the deal yet.

"Herb scolded her," Miriam says. "Go home," he told the dog. "You shouldn't be in the road."

Herb drove on down the road toward the house. "He was going very slowly because he was afraid the dog would run in front of the car again," says Miriam. Instead, it followed the car back to the house.

"Well, you can't just leave the dog on the street," Herb thought, so he looked at her collar. There was a phone number on it. "He put her in the garage and called this phone number," says Miriam. It was the North Shore Animal League. And no, they wouldn't give out the owner's number, but they'd call Herb back when they contacted the owner.

The Phone Rings

The dog spent the day in the garage, and Herb and Miriam brought her water and kept her company. "She was really good," Miriam remembers. "Canny and smart. She never barked at us."

The phone rang. It was the shelter, telling Herb that people on the next street owned the dog. He called the owner, then Herb and Miriam put a rope around the dog's neck and walked her back home.

As it turned out this was the house of the owner's daughter. The owner, a woman of 83, was in the hospital—that was why the dog was staying with the daughter. The dog had jumped the fence because this was one feisty pooch. Hmmm. Herb mulled over the possibilities then quietly said to Miriam, "Maybe we should say we want the dog." They said nothing yet, except that Herb told the owner's daughter, "Let me know what's going to happen to the dog."

Miriam didn't agitate over it, thinking nothing would come of this. "Why would somebody give up their dog," she reasoned.

Next day the owner's daughter called Herb to say in fact mother would like to give up the dog. She had had it only a few months and it was proving too energetic to handle. And as an extra aggravation, the dog had a vexing favorite pastime: running away.

"And that's how we came to get Callie," Miriam says.

Until this moment Miriam had enjoyed the comfortable position of not wanting a dog—but never having to say no outright. Now here was Callie. Seizing the opportunity, Herb made his case convincingly. "Look, we've been married for 56 years," he said. "What new is there to talk about? This would be the new kid in the family."

Thumbs up. Callie was in.

A Dog for the Heart

"I wanted Herb to have something to be happy about," says Miriam. "His strength was fading, his health was ebbing, and I knew it. I wanted this to be a shot in the arm for him. And it was."

Herb and Callie started their daily walks. Soon Herb and his flashy, four-legged companion were striking up conversations with neighbors. "We'd been in the neighborhood for 50 years and some of these people we've never talked to," Miriam found. "But if you walk a dog, you meet people." Callie attracted compliments with her petite, 33-pound physique. "What a beautiful dog," was the common opener. Part sheltie and perhaps collie, Callie's brown topcoat fades into tan as it blends into her short legs. And she has "a fuzzy tail that waves like a sail," as Miriam describes it. "A very pretty dog. If a child wanted to pet Callie, Herb felt so good when the dog behaved and allowed it."

Constant companions, Callie and Herb would sit outside while Herb brushed her every day. When Herb started taking afternoon naps, Callie at first would wait in the kitchen. But then, well, Miriam was out on errands and Herb let Callie know it would be all right to hop in the bed with him. First it was the naps. Pretty soon Callie was tucking in with Herb and Miriam every night.

And though she came cheap to Herb and Miriam, Callie racked up the household bills. Can you expect a dog to go without air conditioning in the summer? Of course not. Though they'd done without central air for all their years in the house, Herb and Miriam installed it now at a cost of $6,500. And is there any question that a dog needs a fence? There you go, for $3,000. "These were Herb's ideas, of course," says Miriam.

From the start Callie knew how to get what she wanted. It was obvious from the way she nabbed Herb. It wasn't long before she hooked Miriam too. When they'd sit down to dinner, Miriam would get up from her seat to serve, "and Callie would immediately jump up into my chair." And if Miriam was comfortably having her dinner when Callie wanted the seat, a dog knows what to do. Go to the door as if you need to go out into the yard, have Miriam get up to let you out—then run back and jump in her chair. Gotcha!

To cinch the Miriam connection, Callie used another cozy-up. To get a treat, go stand by Miriam. If she doesn't oblige, press your face on her knee, so she has to look down at you. If she still doesn't bother to give you something, start barking. "Callie knows how to do wily dog things."

Herb had two regrets about Callie, says Miriam. First, that he never knew her as a puppy. She would have been a beautiful puppy, he knew. Second, "Herb was so enchanted with her, he regretted Callie never had puppies herself. That he didn't have her when she could have had puppies. Of course I was thinking 'thank God.' What would we do with all those puppies?"

No Regrets

Today, with Herb gone, Callie keeps Miriam "busy and occupied." But more than that, Callie is the part of their later life that Miriam has no regrets about. "You know you have regrets about some things. Herb always wanted to go to New York and sleep over, but I always felt that's so ridiculously expensive to stay in those hotels. So we didn't do it. That's my regret."

"But I'm always going to be happy that I let him have the dog. Had I said no, he definitely wouldn't have had her. But I went along with it, and I'll always be grateful that I did."

Truth now, Callie is to Miriam like another child in the family. When Miriam is at Bonnie's house, she'll call Bonnie, Callie—or her granddaughter Rachel, Callie. And at home, Miriam says, "I often call Callie by their names."

And Callie can still put on those dark brown, soulful eyes that make her look pitiful and irresistible. The ones that met Herb's at the car window that May afternoon when Callie found the one who'd been waiting for her for a very long time.

What a Difference a Name Makes

What Mary Remer runs is not a *dog training* school but a *behavioral consulting* business. She doesn't do *obedience* training, she does *companionship* training. There's a difference. And the name it goes by reflects that.

Just as it matters what you call your business, Mary Remer finds it makes a difference what you name your dog.

One thing for sure, there is no better place to be a dog than on the estate in suburban Philadelphia where Mary runs What a Good Dog! Inc. Walk up the stairs to the second floor and on the sunny landing you find Maya, an English bull terrier, stretched out, chin on her paws, basking lazily. Throughout the spread of rooms upstairs, several more English bull terriers amble about freely. Others nestle into billowing, down-filled dog beds in the spacious room where floor-to-ceiling windows overlook acres of green.

All the dogs have nametags. Poptop flops down beside the visitor in the overstuffed armchair. Two yellow Labrador retrievers, Chanson and Toya, sniff out the visitor, then wander off unimpressed.

From the kitchen Mary is giving instructions to a client whose puppy has just completed training. The words "broccoli, leafy greens, bananas, raw food and high-quality kibble" lace the conversation. The topic is diet, but the point is nutritious foods to promote the contented canine.

What a Name Carries

Everything that happens here is about the human-animal relationship. "I think of what we do here as companionship or relationship training. The goal is to have dogs stay in their homes for their whole lives because people understand how to have a successful partnership with them," Mary says. With techniques that capture, lure and shape the desired behavior, What a Good Dog! achieves results that keep Mary's schedule packed with classes and consultations. Some 250 dogs of all varieties come through here each week.

One practical point that distinguishes her training philosophy is this: for behavioral reasons, Mary Remer believes names are important to the dog. "If you have a dog that likes its name, it wants to hear it. It can be a very positive resource in getting the dog to respond."

"I spend a long time naming my puppies," she says of the English bull terriers she breeds. "When you hit the right name, they know it. They want that name. If it's the wrong name, they don't give any response. There's just nothing."

Not that Mary hands out a list of recommended dog names for her clients. Getting the name that fits, well, that's what takes the knowing.

"I don't think my own name fits me, for instance," she notes. "My name is Mary, but most of my friends call me May. It's a name that feels better to me. It's softer. I resonate to it much more. So when these dogs come in, I can be very open to understanding if the dog's name just never clicked," she snaps her fingers.

Jazz? Yes*!*

Take Daisy. "Daisy was a Shetland sheep dog, five months old. The first week the lady brought her in for the six-week training session, I knew right away the dog didn't like its name. Having been raised with animals all my life, I just know."

Say "Daisy" and the dog would give no response. Not the slightest turn of the head. The first week passed. At the second week's training session, the owner was clearly frustrated with the puppy. The breed wasn't new to her. It was the third sheltie the woman had owned, but this time she just couldn't get a connective flow going with the dog.

"Have you considered changing her name? I don't think she likes it," Mary said. The owner was taken by surprise. "Even though we've been calling her Daisy for five months," the woman asked? "Absolutely," Mary said. "She doesn't respond to it anyway."

The owner then asked Mary if any name came to mind. "And just out the blue—I said, 'Jazz.' The woman's chin dropped to the floor. She said, '*I wanted to name her that!* But my friends talked me out of it.'"

"That's the name she wants," Mary said, and explained how to introduce the change.

As soon as the family started calling her Jazz, the dog responded almost instantly. At class the next week, Daisy, now Jazz, was a totally different dog. When called, she came perfectly.

"I think there's a sound vibration that registers with them, for one thing," Mary surmises. "There's softness or hardness to the name. An energy that goes with the sound of anything. 'Daisy' I think of as a generic, nothing-specific kind of name. If I were to think of a Daisy, it would be a yellow female Labrador, slightly overweight, gregarious, really not caring what her name is. Just happy to be here."

In contrast, shelties are either shy and retiring, or they're very bold. "This one was very bold," says Mary. "Daisy just did nothing for her—just didn't speak to her."

Names for All—or Only the Privileged?

Is a "right name" for prima donna pups only? Not at all, as Mary sees it.

Working with a local animal organization, Main Line Rescue, Mary provides training to help abandoned or abused dogs become sociable and adoptable pets. When the car with the rescued dogs pulls up for class each Wednesday, volunteer handlers from What a Good Dog! meet them.

"Some of the dogs come with names that don't fit them, and others have no names," says Mary. So what to call them? "When the dog gets out of the car, we'll look at the dog, and well, you go to your heart and open yourself to the dog," says Mary. "You ask, 'Who are you and what's your name?' And see what comes. We'll start saying names. Eventually somebody comes up with a name—and the dog flicks its head. And that's the name. It may take a week or two, but we always end up with the right name."

Often the rescued dogs are turned in because there was no connection between person and dog, and that disconnect is reflected in the name, as Mary views it. "They got off to the wrong click at the very beginning."

The German shepherd that was picked up wandering around the airport clearly had been somebody's dog. "She knew commands," says Mary. "She knew a lot. But when she would come to school, she was always looking. Always her nose in the air—as if to say, 'Where is my person?' We named her Pearl. She was such a gem. And that was the name for her. It just helped center her. It helped her find some grounding with us. Because her body was here, but her mind and emotional being were out there, wanting to find her people. And it wasn't going to happen. So just to get her to come back in and reconnect, the name was a help."

"I think animals find comfort in the right name."

What the Eyes Say

Comfort, and perhaps identity. So it was with Sage, Mary's bull terrier search-and-rescue dog. Sage wasn't always Sage. Arriving at Mary's as a four-month-old pup, the dog was already dubbed "Twiggy" because she was thin, always moving, burning a lot of calories. "That was her energy."

But in her eyes was something else. "When she got here, we looked at her and said, 'No, not Twiggy.' Her eyes told you she was a wise soul and had work to do. But we had no idea what her work was going to be. So we spent time with her, looked at her, asked her what name she wanted. One day when we were out on the grass with her, one of our assistants said, 'I think she could be Sage.' Boom. She just learned it so fast," says Mary.

As it turned out, Sage did have work to do—work that would call on all her wisdom. "Somebody I work with in search-and-rescue came by and saw special qualities in this dog. We started to train her for search-and-rescue at about a year and a half, and she did really well. She kept on training, and next thing you know she was on a team. Pretty soon we prepared her for cadaver work—above ground, buried and in the water."

"She's very talented, very good," says Mary. "A couple of years ago Sage found two drowning victims from a boat collision off Atlantic City. And after September 11, she worked on the debris there. There's no other bull terrier that's done the search work she has."

The Same by Any Name?

Discerning the name the animal wants versus the one humans like—that's where the art comes in. Toya, a yellow labrador, came all the way from England with her name. The dog liked it, thank you very much, and was totally responsive to being called Toya. But the humans around her didn't take to the name. A move was afoot to change Toya to, well, anything else. New names were tested. "Nothing doing," the dog implied by not responding. Gradually the humans got it. Toya liked her name. "We couldn't change it," says Mary. "She was Toya. Eventually we all came to like it too. That was just her name."

When primatologist Dr. Jane Goodall gave names to the chimps she worked with during her early years in Africa, it set her apart, sometimes for ridicule, in her profession. But of course they have personalities and feelings, Dr. Goodall demurred, so naturally they deserve names.

Mary Remer would say that when it comes to companion animals, they in fact deserve the names *they want*. Get the name right, she finds, and chances are you'll be able to say frequently, "What a good dog!"

Rafting on the River Styx

Dreams come and go, most of them fading with the morning light. But this one lingers for Steve, every detail vivid in his memory all these years later.

Gargoyle was in it. So was Asia.

Gargoyle and Asia, no figments spun in a fleeting dream, were Steve's hulky, 80-poundish, real life dogs—shar-peis, the Chinese breed with the wrinkly face. First came Gargoyle, Steve's companion for 11 years. Then Asia, who arrived after Gargoyle's time.

The two dogs never met, except in the dream of the river Styx. The real river Styx cascades down a mountainside to a deep gorge in northern Greece. But in classical mythology it was the crossroads to the world of the dead. The river Styx formed the boundary to the realm of Hades, the underworld. Souls were ferried across by Charon, the boatman, usually portrayed as a coarse, bearded old man. Charon would accept for passage only those souls who had received funeral rites and had the proper toll: a small gold coin.

Before the dream, Steve knew nothing of the river Styx. Maybe a smattering of some Greek mythology back in school days, but he had no abiding interest in the subject. He's a chiropractor, not a classicist. His bliss and what he's known for is hands-on work: he is a chiropractor for dogs.

But after the dream Steve awoke, hugged Asia who was sleeping on his bed, and looked at her with a new appreciation.

Asia wasn't Gargoyle, never had been, and that was the problem.

Special from the Start

Gargoyle could have no replacement, after all. He was Steve's first dog. Steve was working as a veterinary technician back then, just about to move out of his family home and get a dog of his own. One of the breeders who came to the vet's office was awaiting the birth of a litter of puppies and Steve placed his name on the list. They were shar-peis. "I got attracted to the breed. They're smart and interesting."

But it was to be a litter of one. Gargoyle came out first, extra large, and acted as a cork preventing the other pups from being born. The breeder thought the best home for this lone survivor would be with Steve.

"My special buddy" from the start, as Steve puts it, Gargoyle and he went everywhere together. Besides Gargoyle, Steve had two Boston terriers. But Gargoyle wasn't a people dog or a dog's dog. He was Steve's dog and pretty much only Steve's dog. "He didn't bond with other people or animals. He wouldn't come up to you and wag his tail. He was really aloof."

It's no mystery why Gargoyle attached with a passion to Steve. Gargoyle had health problems from day one because of the difficulty of his birth, and he wasn't a happy-face dog. Steve tended him with meticulous attention. "I really couldn't walk him; he'd get colitis if he went for a walk. So we drove around together." On errands. On visits to friends. And every day Gargoyle went to work with Steve at the vet's office.

For 11 years they were side by side.

"I thought I'd have him a lot longer, but he swallowed a toy, and I didn't realize it. Shortly afterward, he started getting sick. I kept taking him to the vet. We'd do tests and found nothing wrong. Maybe he's just getting older, the vet said. Steve took Gargoyle back a third time and said, "I think there is something seriously wrong."

Sure enough, a barium x-ray found a shadow in Gargoyle's stomach. The stomach was in fact beginning to twist in on itself, something that can cause fatal bloating. The vet surmised it was likely a tumor and he'd do surgery. But if it was a tumor, "We won't wake him up," the vet said.

Steve waited. A half hour later the vet came out laughing. In his hand he was holding a toy—swallowed by Gargoyle and now safely removed. "He's going to be fine," the vet said. Two days later, Steve took Gargoyle home. But the dog wouldn't eat. Steve came home from work that night to find Gargoyle lying flat out, "like a limp doll." "I'm bringing him right over," he told the vet.

The vet hooked him up to an IV, did an EKG and performed all manner of heroic measures. But Gargoyle didn't make it.

The Solution: Another Shar-pei

As emotional a blow as it was to Steve, Gargoyle's passing changed things on a practical level at the house too. A fierce watchdog, Gargoyle was far more intimidating than the two small Boston terriers could ever be. The fierce-looking

Gargoyle barked and kept out intruders in this rough-and-getting-rougher neighborhood. Steve had never had a problem with thieves. In fact he'd leave the house unlocked. But the day after Gargoyle died, someone broke into the backyard and stole a bicycle.

The solution: another shar-pei, Steve decided, and he immediately set out to find one. Posting messages on vet clinic bulletin boards, he didn't expect an instant response because this is not a common breed. But by the time Steve got home, he had two messages. One was about a female shar-pei-lab mix named Asia—now in a shelter and scheduled to be put down the next day. Steve called, got a quick description and went off to see her.

Gargoyle had been gone only a week.

"I knew I was going to adopt Asia, sight unseen. But when I got to the shelter and saw her, I found she was a magnificent dog. Beautiful and statuesque. She looked like a black lab but had the big shar-pei face, full of wrinkles—a really striking dog."

Steve went home with Asia. "But it was really too soon after Gargoyle. I was so close to Gargoyle that Asia was just a daily reminder that I didn't have Gargoyle anymore. It was tough to bond with her."

"When you adopt a stray from the pound, you never know how old they are. They thought Asia was about two," says Steve. Likely it was a brutal two years, if the bullet in her was any indication. Never removed, it was probably birdshot that wouldn't penetrate. Besides the bullet, Asia had every kind of worm and a scraggly coat. "Her food preference when she arrived was grubs and mice—vestiges of her survival methods," Steve says.

Despite the hardscrabble history, Asia loved people and came with a wonderful temperament. As for other dogs, that was different matter. All were utterly contemptible in Asia's view. "In dog life there is a hierarchy," Steve observes. "There is royalty and there are peasants. Asia was royalty." That meant Asia ruled the now-five-dog household. Besides the two terriers there was a crippled dalmatian, with whom Asia was actually close, and another shar-pei. Marking territory, challenging every upstart canine insurrection, Asia was the uber-empress of this dog world. So much so that Steve started taking Asia everywhere with him. She relished being the only dog, and it gave the other dogs a break.

Four years passed. Steve comfortably accepted Asia as part of his life now. But she was never quite Gargoyle.

Then came this dream.

Passage Denied

"We were in the river Styx, floating on a raft. Me, Asia, and my dalmatian, Jackson. Everything in the dream was in a grayish-green color. Even the water, and the dead people along the sides of the river. Even we were."

"Then I looked over and noticed Gargoyle standing on the bank of the river. He was glowing in a whitish-cream color, the same color he was in real life. There was a light all around him, while everything else was gray-green. He was like an alive dog. He was vibrant. He looked happy, and had a grin on his face."

"Asia then jumped off the raft, got into the river and swam over to the bank. She stood there next to Gargoyle. And as she was standing there, Asia started to turn to stone. She was becoming a grayish color, like granite."

"Gargoyle then looked at Asia and shook his head at her. With that, Asia jumped back into the river and then turned black again—her natural color. She swam over to us and got back on the raft."

"We paddled away from the river Styx and went the opposite direction, back to this world. That was the end of the dream."

"When I woke up, I felt nothing but dread. I was glad to see Gargoyle again, even if it was a dream. But at the same time I felt this fear regarding Asia. I hugged her (all my dogs sleep with me), and from that day on I appreciated her in a much deeper way. We got very close. Because something told me I wasn't going to have her much longer."

Shortly after that Asia started having strange health problems. Her legs swelled—from a disease shar-peis get rather commonly. But because she was a mixed breed, neither the vets nor Steve quite put it together. Different vets looked her over, took x-rays, found an infection and treated her with antibiotics. It was resolved. Asia was fine again.

One night Steve took Asia with him to a picnic at a friend's house. It was dark by then, and Asia banged into a few people, quite unlike her. Steve took her to the vet. Asia, it seems, was now blind in one eye. "Still, I didn't think anything of it."

Every so often now, Asia wouldn't be herself.

A year passed. Asia was seven years old, maybe older. "One night I came home from a movie and found Asia with her whole face swollen, and her feet swollen. I thought she'd been stung by something. So I called my vet in the middle of the night, and his associate agreed to meet me. She was really worried. Here I was thinking Asia'd been stung by a bee or a spider and she'd get a shot and we'd go home. But the vet told me all Asia's organs had shut down. They'd stopped working."

"I was stunned. She said there was nothing that could be done, and should she put her down? I said I'm not prepared to say goodbye yet."

Steve took Asia home. He contacted a vet friend, a holistic practitioner, hoping there was a remedy yet. The friend saw Asia and said, no, she didn't feel there was anything that could be done. They put her on an IV to maintain her comfort. The vet called an internist and discussed Asia's case. What they felt was that she had a disease common to shar-peis—amyloidosis. A protein storage disease, it at some point switches on a gene that manufactures protein in tremendous amounts and clogs up the organs.

The symptoms Asia had been having all along were that disease process getting started. There was really no way out of this, and "they almost begged me to put her to sleep," Steve says.

With New Appreciation

It was no easier losing Asia than Gargoyle—because after the dream "our last year together was great."

Amyloidosis, Steve points out, almost mimics the stone-like transformation of Asia in the dream. "It gets into the little spaces inside organs and stiffens up the works."

"When Gargoyle shook his head at Asia in the dream, I felt it was his way of saying to Asia, 'No, go back, it's not your time yet.'"

"And I felt it was Gargoyle's way of saying to me, Asia's not going to be here much longer—but Gargoyle was going to be there to help."

"I think there's a much deeper bond between us and animals than we realize. We love them, we're attached to them in life, and there are bonds that go so deep we don't even understand."

"I'm not a religious person, but it gave me hope that death isn't final and that we can be there for each other. That dogs and animals are part of the afterlife, and that we're all going to be reunited somehow."

Today Steve's professional card for his chiropractic practice carries this logo: two dogs—Gargoyle and Asia—on either side of Steve's name. "They kind of remind me of the Foo dogs in Chinese mythology. A male and a female facing each other, protecting their surroundings."

"What's bizarre about that dream," Steve sees, "is that every other dream fades over time. But this one never does."

The Dog in the Window

It was late, near midnight on a white Christmas, when Judith and Marty Miller rounded the corner to their house on Dove Lane. From the top of their driveway, Marty braked carefully down the steep, snowy slope.

The sliding glass door of their contemporary house came into sight, and there they saw him. Sitting in the front hall, waiting. He was, as Judith recalls, "looking out at us," a light glowing from behind.

Their Irish water spaniel, Chewie. "Oh, no, he got out of the kitchen," Judith groaned. "The house is going to be destroyed!" Marty echoed, "Oh, my gosh."

On the way out that morning they had left Chewie, a few months old, in the kitchen with food and water. They carefully locked the dog gate that led from the kitchen into the front hall.

It wasn't an easy choice for the Millers, but it was that or miss Christmas with their son and his family who lived in a New York high-rise. No dogs allowed.

"I was nervous about Chewie being alone that very long day," Judith says. "But at least he was safely confined to the kitchen and wasn't going to destroy the house by the time we got back. Still, he'd never been left this long before."

Reckless as any puppy, Chewie would surely delight in this breakout opportunity to rip, chew and knock over whatever he pleased. What would be the scene here now, Judith imagined, after a long day and evening of this wreckage?

Expecting the worst, Judith and Marty approached the front door.

But the front hall, where they had seen Chewie through the glass door, was empty. No dog.

Still in the Kitchen

They looked into the kitchen and there, still locked behind the gate, jumping at the sight of them, was Chewie.

"I burst into tears," says Judith, "because I knew that it was Meatball we saw in the window. Chewie and Meatball looked exactly alike."

Meatball? "He was the dog we had before Chewie."

Meatball had died the summer before.

It wasn't the first time Meatball had made his influence known after his demise. Something of him seemed to survive the most formidable barriers, including a hurricane. Marty and Judith had buried Meatball on a dune in front of their beach house at the New Jersey shore. Their companion of 13 years, he was family and they didn't let go of his memory easily. With ceremony, they marked Meatball's grave with stones, with his food bowl—and placed a feather on the spot.

Not long after, a hurricane blew through. Judith drove to the shore house as soon as she could to see if there had been any damage. Walking out to Meatball's grave site, she expected no trace of the mementos they'd placed there. Then her eyes spotted it: the feather—and only the feather—still standing.

Over the years Meatball had become deeply ensconced in the Millers' lives, so replacing him wasn't the most natural thing to do at first. They waited several months. Then came Chewie.

From the start Marty affectionately called Chewie a "special needs" dog. Chewie had allergies and lost much of his fur. He would sometimes pitch into a frenzy, racing about, pounding his tail against the wall to the point where it would bleed. He had two operations on his tail.

The Constant Companion

But, no problem, Chewie endeared himself to the Millers and became Judith's nosing, nuzzling companion, even at work. A psychologist, therapist and teacher, Judith had Chewie at her feet when she saw clients in her therapy practice at home. Wherever Judith went, Chewie trotted alongside.

For nine years, they were family. Then, brushing Chewie one day, Judith felt a lump on his neck. It was a lymphoma. The vet convinced Judith that chemotherapy would give him a good chance of getting better.

"It worked for a while," she says, "then it didn't." Desperate to turn things around, Judith was giving him medicine, making him pot roast and chicken, whatever he would eat. "It was heartbreaking," she recalls.

Chewie became more and more dependent on Judith as the disease advanced. "He was constantly on my mind."

When it was clear that Chewie was not doing well, but there was still hope, Judith had a dream. The setting: the vet's office, where she'd taken her dogs for 20 years. "I was hugging the vet, Dr. Denby, and we were both crying. We were saying goodbye to each other, because he said he was moving away," she recalls of the dream.

A month later, the dream scene came to life. "I actually was in the vet's office and the same scene took place. It had become clear chemo was not working for Chewie. The vet and I were both crying. They loved Chewie there. Dr. Denby and I were hugging each other."

"The only piece of the dream that wasn't true in this real life scene," she notes, "was the reason for saying goodbye. It was not because the vet was moving away."

What the vet did say that day in the office was that no more treatment was appropriate. It would be best just to take Chewie home. Yes, said Judith, that was exactly what she wanted to do. Slowly she walked Chewie to the car and they went home. "I gave him pills that would make him feel more comfortable, and whatever else he wanted." As he weakened and lost interest in food, she started feeding him drops of liquid food in his water.

They layered a soft bed for him in the bedroom.

The Call of the Tree

Come a Saturday in February, Judith held a long-scheduled weekend holotropic breathing workshop in her home. In this form of therapy, participants lie on the floor on comfortable blankets for several hours. Evocative music plays and dream images emerge for the participants, who are in a deep state of repose. From these images Judith and each client later glean patterns and insights.

That day, Chewie lay on the floor peacefully alongside the participants. "Everyone there knew Chewie," Judith says. "He was there in his own bed, with his music and his friends."

When the breathwork was over, she moved Chewie into the bedroom where he could look out through the glass doors into the woods.

"Then I noticed something strange," Judith says. "As Chewie was lying there, and could hardly move, he would lift up his head and stretch his neck toward that big tree outside the window."

"I thought at first that he saw something. It was amazing. He couldn't move, but he was stretching out with his head toward the tree."

A few days later Chewie took a disturbing turn. He started vibrating, as in a seizure.

Judith called the vet's office. They said, "Well, as long as he's comfortable." Comfortable??? The seizure passed. But Tuesday night a second one came. Judith called the vet. No answer. She massaged Chewie. He finally went to sleep.

Next morning at seven another seizure, this one frighteningly violent, gripped the dog. Judith called the vet's office, begging for someone to come and help her lift Chewy and take him there.

No, the office didn't offer house calls or that service, she was told. And Dr. Denby was out of town. Call our backup vet, or a transport service, was their response. "You can't do that," Judith said. "This dog is in agony, having seizures." Well, this is the number to call for the transport service. Judith called. She got a recorded message.

Trying to lift the dog, and unable, and Marty away, Judith called Chewie's dog sitter, their friend, Julie, who came rushing over. But even together they couldn't carry him. Frantic now, Judith called Joe, a contractor who had become a friend over the years and had unfailingly helped the Millers when they most needed it. It was snowing. Joe came with a co-worker. Judith wrapped Chewie in a blanket and the two big men carried him out to the car and to the vet's office.

"And there, after I hugged Chewie and held him, they did what they do," she ends the story.

Packing Away the Grief

The day after Chewie died, Judith got up early, crying, not having slept at all. Adding to the grief was anger at the callous behavior from her vet's office during Chewie's final hours. But it was a work day and she was scheduled to teach at Columbia. Grief packed inside, she drove to the train and went to New York.

"Somehow I got through what I had to go through. I turned off my grief."

By end of day, a blizzard had begun. Back in Philadelphia, Judith inched her way home on a snow-blanketed expressway, wind swirling and visibility near zero. When she pulled up to the house, it was 11 p.m. By now a depleted woman, she got out of the car at the top of the driveway.

"I couldn't safely drive down the hill—it was ice all the way," she remembers. "I walked cautiously down to the house—and I fell. My books spilled down the hill. So I did the only thing I could do: I just sat there and cried."

In the house now, Judith "for some reason" went to the computer. "I don't know why, given that I was beside myself. Maybe just to clear my mind, I checked my e-mails."

Along with the junk and the can-waits, was one surprise. An e-mail from Lois, a past client in Judith's breathwork practice. More than a year had passed since Judith had seen her. Lois had also been a student of Judith's at a local college where Judith taught. Lois had tried one breathwork session, but as an abuse victim, she found the imagery it evoked too frightening, Judith recalls. "So we kind of wrapped it up and I said, if ever you want to come back . . . ."

Lois graduated from college and there had been no contact since.

But tonight came this e-mail from Lois. "Dear Dr. Miller," she began. "I hope you won't mind my sending you this e-mail, but you've been on my mind so much this last week. These last few weeks, she continued, I've had dreams of you and just felt like I should call you—even though I don't know why. So I put it off," she wrote in her message.

"I Had This Dream"

"Then," Lois went on, "I had this dream last night. It was a dream that I really want to share with you. I don't know why but it seems really important to do."

Judith offers this quick background. "In the breathwork Lois did with me, which was so scary for her, the central image was a tree. A very large tree. But there were no leaves on it. A barren, naked tree. As I recall in the breathwork, Lois was somehow going toward it or looking at it—and a big vulture flew out of the tree and tried to attack her. And then everything went black. Black sky, black tree, all of it black."

"That was her very frightening breathwork experience; it recalled the terrorizing experience of her abuse," Judith recaps.

Lois reviewed all of that for Judith in the e-mail, just to remind her. Then Lois recounted her dream of the night before. "In the dream I had last night, there was another tree. It was a beautiful, big tree."

"Somehow I was looking at it, stretching my head, staring at this tree. And from behind the tree came this beautiful, beautiful light. Suddenly I found myself under the tree, embracing it in soft moss, feeling comfort, safety and light all around me. And I knew nothing could hurt me. I was in a place where I knew I'd never have problems again. For some reason, it felt really important to tell you this."

Lois had known nothing of Chewie's illness, his death the day before, or his pulling toward the tree in his final days.

"All I can tell you is I felt so happy," Judith says. "Chewie had come through Lois—she was the messenger. I can never thank her enough for what she gave me."

Did it change Judith's experience of grief over Chewie? "Permanently," she nods. "It brought me comfort. I loved that screwy dog so much. I was so devastated when he suffered."

And Lois? "I never heard from her again," Judith says. "That was the last exchange we had. That snowy night when I came home so completely beside myself. She sent me that e-mail on Thursday. Chewie had died on Wednesday."

Why would Lois, a distant figure in Chewie's and Judith's life, experience this connecting dream? "I don't know," Judith admits. "She didn't have any special relationship with Chewie, but she had met him. And Lois did love animals. She had several of her own."

Transformation—or coincidence? Was Lois's dream a spontaneous natural resolution of childhood trauma? Was Chewie's effort in stretching his neck toward the tree, staring intently in his final hours, just a neurological quirk?

What Judith does know is that transformation of the kind suggested in Lois' dream—the earlier image of an attacking vulture swooping out of a barren tree before all turned to blackness being converted into a new image of a green and soft place drenched in light—is the core of what Judith attempts in her life's work.

"The idea," she says of her work, "is to develop ourselves to a point where we can feel closer to that divinity that we're a part of. That's what I've done in my life—to try to assist people in reaching their potential to recognize themselves as spiritual beings. I try to do that in my practice, in my teaching, my writing, just living my life."

For Chewie to be in on the mystery—mesmerized by the tree, and pulling his near-lifeless neck to full stretch toward it in his final hours—well, Judith is awed.

Judith observes in her therapeutic practice of 25 years, "even with people in the field of psychology or in academia, people from a purely rational tradition, all I have to do is open up the arena to assist them in tapping those parts of themselves. And invariably they're eager to go there."

She settles back. "The truth I see is that we're all connected. It goes beyond who we are as individuals. There's pain, but there are miracles and wonders too. It's all a continuum. Life and death are a circle that keeps moving. These experiences with Chewie, and others, have affirmed this belief for me and given me a lot of personal peace."

Elinor Donahue is a freelance business writer based in Philadelphia. She has published numerous articles on animal-related subjects and a weekly newspaper column for the placement of shelter animals. She can be reached at ElinorDonahue@comcast.net.

Printed in the USA
CPSIA information can be obtained
at www.ICGtesting.com
LVHW090330070324
773789LV00029B/442

9 781599 264141